The Pulse of Contemporary Turkish

Middle East Literature in Translation
Michael Beard and Adnan Haydar, *Series Editors*

Select Titles in Middle East Literature in Translation

Allah's Spacious Earth
Omar Sayfo; Paul Olchváry, trans.

A Cup of Sin: Selected Poems
Simin Behbahani; Farzaneh Milani and Kaveh Safa, trans.

The House of the Edrisis: A Novel, Volume One
Ghazaleh Alizadeh; M. R. Ghanoonparvar, trans.

The House of the Edrisis: A Novel, Volume Two
Ghazaleh Alizadeh; M. R. Ghanoonparvar, trans.

Salt Journals: Tunisian Women on Political Imprisonment
Haifa Zangana, Christalla Yakinthou, and Virginie Ladisch, eds.; Katharine Halls and Nariman Youssef, trans.

In Search of Walid Masoud: A Novel
Jabra Ibrahim Jabra; Roger Allen and Adnan Haydar, trans.

Sour Grapes
Zakaria Tamer; Alessandro Columbu and Mireia Costa Capallera, trans.

We Never Swim in the Same River Twice
Hassouna Mosbahi; William Maynard Hutchins, trans.

For a full list of titles in this series, visit https://press.syr.edu/supressbook-series/middle-east-literature-in-translation/.

The Pulse of Contemporary Turkish

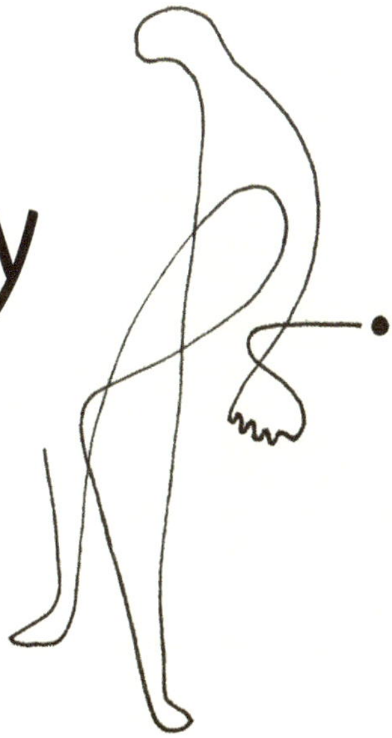

Poems from the New Millennium

Selected and translated from the Turkish by

Buğra Giritlioğlu with **Daniel Scher**

Foreword by **Laurent Mignon**

Syracuse University Press

Syracuse University Press
Syracuse, New York 13244-5290

First Edition 2025

25 26 27 28 29 30 6 5 4 3 2 1

The drawing on the title page is by Anita Sezgener.

For a listing of books published and distributed by Syracuse University Press, visit https://press.syr.edu.

ISBN: 9780815638629 (paperback)
9780815657408 (e-book)

Library of Congress Cataloging-in-Publication Data

Names: Giritlioğlu, Buğra, editor, translator. | Scher, Daniel, editor, translator. | Mignon, Laurent, 1971– writer of foreword.

Title: The pulse of contemporary Turkish : poems from the new millennium / selected and translated from the Turkish by Buğra Giritlioğlu with Daniel Scher ; foreword by Laurent Mignon.

Description: First edition. | Syracuse, New York : Syracuse University Press, 2025. | Series: Middle East literature in translation

Identifiers: LCCN 2025000935 (print) | LCCN 2025000936 (ebook) | ISBN 9780815638629 (paperback) | ISBN 9780815657408 (ebook)

Subjects: LCSH: Turkish poetry—21st century—Translations into English.

Classification: LCC PL271.E3 P85 2025 (print) | LCC PL271.E3 (ebook) | DDC 894/.351408—dc23/eng/20250131

LC record available at https://lccn.loc.gov/2025000935

LC ebook record available at https://lccn.loc.gov/2025000936

The authorized representative in the EU for product safety and compliance is Mare Nostrum Group B.V.
Mauritskade 21D, 1091 GC Amsterdam, The Netherlands
gpsr@mare-nostrum.co.uk

For Philip Esposito (Sör/Espo)
and the late Chilton Watrous (Miss Watrous),
my prep-year English teachers.

It was through your tireless "soliloquies" that
this great language slowly grew intelligible to my ears.

And for my classmates,
including those I locked horns with
during fierce English spelling bees that year.

It turns out I was going away to fall in love . . .
If a soothsayer had told me so in advance, I surely would not have tried to go back, but maybe I would have upset the sequence of events and turned time topsy-turvy by obsessing over where and how I would encounter this love. What draws us into time is not knowing our future. Otherwise, waiting in the knowledge that one day she will undress as soon as her knees are touched would be beyond the patience of a mortal.

—Melih Cevdet Anday, *Raziye*
(translated from the Turkish by Buğra Giritlioğlu, with Daniel Scher)

The reading of the poets had still more overpowering effects; I am not sure that the discovery of love is necessarily more exquisite than the discovery of poetry. Poetry transformed me: initiation into death itself will not carry me farther along into another world than does a dusk of Virgil. . . . The most complicated and most obscure poets have pleased me above all; they force my thought to strenuous exercise; I have sought, too, the latest and the oldest, those who open wholly new paths, or help me to find lost trails.

—Marguerite Yourcenar, *Memoirs of Hadrian*
(translated from the French by Grace Frick in collaboration with the author)

Contents

Foreword

Laurent Mignon

"We've had it with the rose, the nightingale, the soul, the moonshine, and all that," wrote Nâzım Hikmet (1902–63) in a poem that he was to include in *Varan 3* (1930), one of his early collections.[1] At the time, the young man, a convinced socialist, was designing an avant-gardist poetry meant both to break with the past and to shape the future. However, his call was not solely an invitation to fellow poets to do away with the mystique and mystifications of classical Ottoman poetry. Few were those still perpetuating the divan tradition and exploring its mystical subtext in the literary Istanbul of the early years of the republic. Hikmet's anger was directed as well at the representation of Turkey in Western literatures, what he called elsewhere "the Orient of the books."[2]

To read his verses almost a century after they were written is also an invitation for us to reflect upon the image of Turkish poetry, old and new, created in English-language anthologies. Could it not be argued that in this context, too, an "Orient of the anthologies" was constructed? This "Orient" took various forms. Sometimes the emphasis was on continuity among Ottoman court poetry, folk tradition, and modern poetry in approaches that were not devoid of essentialist premises. In other cases, the focus was on dichotomies:

1. Nâzım Hikmet, "Promete, Pipomuz, Gül, Bülbül vs.," in *Bütün Şiirleri*, ed. Güven Turan and Fahri Güllüoğlu (Istanbul: Yapı Kredi, 2007), 128.

2. Nâzım Hikmet, "Piyer Loti," in *Bütün Şiirleri*, 34.

East and West, old and new, folk and classical. Not that these issues are insignificant, but are they all that matters?

It is true that after the second half of the nineteenth century, a critical engagement with the past and a literary engagement with modernity were uppermost in poets' minds as they explored new ideas and novel ways to express them. In later years, some poets put more personal, existential interrogations at the forefront of their poetic forays: metaphysical anguish with a "Baudelairian" touch in some of Yahya Kemal's (1884–1958) neoclassical verse, melancholic longing in Ahmet Haşim's (1887–1933) symbolist poetry, or, indeed, spiritual yearnings in Asaf Halet Çelebi's (1907–58) avant-gardist works. Nonetheless, most of the poetry of the early republican period was above all a poetry of ideas—nationalist, socialist, or religious—and, later, a poetry about the little things in life, as defined in the manifesto of the Garip (Bizarre, Forlorn) movement penned by Orhan Veli (1914–50) and published in 1941. The 1950s witnessed a dramatic change with the advent of a movement that critics would retrospectively call İkinci Yeni (Second New). These poets brought to the fore the complexities of human existence, while making full use of all opportunities offered by the Turkish language in modernist poems that challenged the populist status quo. One can argue that İkinci Yeni constituted, to paraphrase the personalist philosopher Emmanuel Mounier (1905–50) on the genesis of existentialist philosophies, *a poetry of humans as a reaction against the excesses of the poetry of ideas and the poetry of things.*[3] The exploration of existentialist themes, in the broadest sense of the term, and an imagist sensitivity were at the heart of this new poetry whose foremost advocates, including Turgut Uyar (1927–85), Cemal Süreya (1931–90), and Gülten Akın (1933–2015), among many others, were not necessarily aware that they were part of a new movement. Unlike the Garip group, the İkinci Yeni poets never published a common manifesto advancing their perspective on life and poetry.

3. Emmanuel Mounier, *Existentialist Philosophies: An Introduction*, trans. Eric Blow (London: Rockliff, 1948), 2.

Of course, much would happen between the late 1950s and the 2000s, on which the current anthology focuses. Yet one can argue that the poetry of the İkinci Yeni forms the matrix of contemporary Turkish poetry. The early years of the twenty-first century were characterized by an abundance of manifestos that mapped the tensions between conflicting understandings of poetry, fluctuating among the lyrical, the political, and the experimental. The extent to which such texts affected the poetry scene of our times is open to debate. What does strike readers of poetry of the new millennium, however, is an increased concern with existential themes in addition to love, a perennial topic in the poetry of Turkish-speaking lands, and nature, a relatively new theme in the context of Turkish poetry. Thus, it was more than appropriate that Buğra Giritlioğlu, as he skimmed the extensive corpus of poems, selected those that engaged with such themes as life, death, love, time, and nature for inclusion in this volume. Not only do these themes represent the major concerns of today's poets, but Giritlioğlu's approach has also a philosophical pertinence. Indeed, he de-orientalizes Turkish poetry as he explores, by way of his selection of poems and poets, the universality of contemporary verse. In vain will readers look for a *nightingale* in this selection, though they will encounter a *thrush* in a poem by Lâle Müldür and meet several poets evoking the *rose*. Readers will even come across the "lost *souls* the future disperses through history" (italics added) in verses by Murathan Mungan and a *moon* that "resembled a closed parenthesis" in a poem by Miray Çakıroğlu. But those roses, souls, and moons are not necessarily of the type that Nâzım Hikmet condemned. These images are subverted and appropriated in manifold attempts to express the multiplicity of human experiences in poetic form.

Buğra Giritlioğlu's volume *The Pulse of Contemporary Turkish: Poems from the New Millennium* is thus a unique and much-needed introduction to the diversity of the poetry scene in Turkey. Moreover, centering around universal themes, it is also a powerful antidote against the identitarian drifts characteristic of our age.

A Glance at Contemporary Poetry in Turkish

Ecotonal Poetry

Ayşegül Tözeren

Translated by Kenan Behzat Sharpe, Daniel Scher, and Buğra Giritlioğlu

Before many of the contributors to this anthology were even born, the influential Turkish poet Atillâ İlhan (1925–2005) wrote:

> festivities have subsided, all that remains in the garden is a bitter
> breeze
> that song in *maqam mahûr* plays, müjgân and i weep
> friends have departed the feast has ended neither the old joy nor
> speed.[1]

These lines might as well describe the landscape in which contemporary Turkish-language poetry was born: it all emerged after the feast had ended. Although the age range of the authors in this

1. A *maqam* (Turkish: *makam*) is a melodic mode used as a basis for improvisation or composition in Persian, Arabic, and Turkish music. *Mahur,* which roughly corresponds to the European G-major scale, is generally regarded as an uplifting *maqam.* The average Turkish speaker would assume "müjgân" was a person because it is a common woman's name. In fact, it was the poet's cat. The Persian-derived word means "eyelash," though few Turkish speakers would know that today.

anthology is rather wide (thirty-one to seventy-three), most of the poems were written in only the past twenty years.

The past four decades saw several pivotal events that greatly influenced the trajectory of Turkish poetry. A regime of censorship ensued in the wake of a coup by the Turkish military in 1980. Strangely enough, this was accompanied by a rise in free-market economics, which dominated the 1990s—political repression juxtaposed with economic liberalization. It was very difficult to discuss social issues, yet individuals were free and, indeed, encouraged to disclose details of their private life. During this same period, the reality of being able to watch a war, the Gulf War, unfold on the increasingly widespread color television dropped like a cannonball into people's living rooms. The zeitgeist of the country had just become stranger.

The poems featured in these pages were born into this outlandish climate. In terms of lineage, they did not retain the features of what immediately preceded them. They instead leaped back to the poetry of the 1950s, carrying that period's features to extremes and propelling them over the threshold of the 2000s. The resulting poetry exploited the associativity that characterized the 1950s but with word associations now bordering on mental flight. The basic building block of poetry grew ever finer: first the individual line, later the word, and today the syllable, letter, symbol, and sound. As the existential universe became more chaotic, what stood out went far beyond the inward retreat of existentialism—a schizophrenic language that represented a folding in on oneself. In these poems, the inner voice dominates. However, owing to the dilemma-ridden 1990s, this inner voice has no outside: cocooning itself while putting all on display, like a turtle without a shell. The inner voice dissipates, floats about, and has no concern for matters such as consistency. It creates an aesthetics of chaos and noise.

With the advent of the new millennium, the end of history is declared, and the tickets for grand narratives held in the poet's hand expire. But poets tend to scrape the inauthentic, exposing truth. With traces of modernism and postmodernism still palpable in their work, today's poets, searching for the kernel of truth, suddenly realize that both the end and the death of history have been proclaimed. The pendulum keeps swinging between modernism and postmodernism. With its insides hollowed out, the past, reduced to a mere excerpt in quotes, consists of little more than a feeling of nostalgia.

Poets are now those who cannot return home. Swaying between modernist exuberance and postmodernist irony, they write in an era in which history accelerates nonstop. As they compose, they do not look at paper; their fingertips are on plastic keys, their eyes on a computer screen. Paper is an empty space that whets the imagination, whereas behind the Word document there are any number of windows—opening, closing, winking. It's impossible for the poet to escape. With what the British cultural critic Alan Kirby calls "digimodernism" leaking from those windows, the poet writes at the bottom of a cultural chasm where populism reigns supreme and hate speech is mistaken for courage.[2]

Poets can stare that chasm in the eye and descend into their own hell. They recognize that those who fail to see their own hell cannot reach the true concern and, yes, object of poetry. Every time poets seek to unearth their life's essence and bring it onto the page, they will look back and converse with the past, whether it be with sincerity or irony. This is the desire that burns (in) everything they write, summoning them again and again to write even better.

In Buğra Giritlioğlu's anthology, the poets' footpaths into their respective hells lead to the universal themes of life, death, love, time, and nature. Examining the architecture of the texts reveals a diversity of voices, raised in response to the impositions of the age. Through the use of various forms, the poets react to the dizzying speed, information bombardment, class injustices, and speciesism of the present day. The selected poems not only push the limits of the imagination but also violate the boundaries of literary genres, creating themselves anew in ecotones. Some of the poems also incorporate

2. Alan Kirby, *Digimodernism: How New Technologies Dismantle the Postmodern and Reconfigure Our Culture* (New York: Continuum, 2009).

visual elements, which is often dismissed as an "experimental pursuit." But classifying poets according to how they construct their aesthetic design amounts to boxing them into little playgrounds—and that does not mesh with the free spirit of poetry.

We know that in every region and every century, poets will explore different worlds and summon their readers there. We also know that poets will translate the world they inhabit into the language of their poetics, thereby creating a new world. And when asked whether the question is *to be or not to be*, they will always point to some other possibility.

This anthology, far removed from the turbulence of dualities, seeks its readers from among those who have their eyes fixed on that other possibility.

Turkish Poetry since 2000

Utku Özmakas

Translated by Kenan Behzat Sharpe,
Daniel Scher, and Buğra Giritlioğlu

Historical Roots

The primary reference for post-2000 Turkish poetry is the İkinci Yeni (Second New) movement (1950 to mid-1960s), considered one of the pinnacles of the genre. Unlike its precursor, now referred to as the Birinci Yeni (First New) movement, which advocated a colloquial, narrative style, Second New pursued an image-based poetics and went beyond the quotidian, expanding poetry's thematic scope.[1] Many critics of the time dismissed Second New poetry as "meaningless" or "formalist," not appreciating the meanings its practitioners found outside the bounds of conventional language.

The second waymark in the evolution of poetry in the 2000s can best be expressed as a *via negativa:* poets of the 1980s largely freed themselves from the combative, political language of the 1970s. They transformed the "agitprop" and socialist poetry of the 1970s, accusing the previous generation of "sloganeering." Poetry of the 1980s

1. Christened "Garip" (Bizarre) by its founders in 1941 to reappropriate the way others viewed its members' poems and poetic ideals, the movement was called "First New" only in retrospect, after the emergence of Second New. (Garip poets also embraced the other meaning of *garip*, "forlorn"—their poetry often dealing with troubles of the little guy.)

inherited and overinvested in the imagist legacy of Second New, while striving to make poetry more reader-friendly and accessible. This poetic language also defined the 1990s.

A Map of the 2000s

Journals

Turkey was home to more than two hundred literary journals at the start of the new millennium, with more than one hundred of them dedicated solely to poetry. What led to this flourishing? The obvious answer is the ease of digital publishing and the concomitant advent of electronic journals. These factors, coupled with the difficulty young poets faced in breaking into the conservative mainstream, prompted them to seek and launch new literary venues.

Although these numbers may suggest a thriving literary scene, low print runs and distribution issues prevented most of these journals from achieving recognition on a national scale. Moreover, the plethora of journal titles portended that the raft of new poetry would eventually run aground. Nevertheless, some niche magazines did at least compel larger literary outlets to take notice of "experimental poetry."

Manifestos

The 2000s also saw a boom of poetry manifestos. The Madde Akımı (Materials Movement) manifesto of 2004 by Cem Kurtuluş and Efe Murad was born of an exhibit organized by the two high school friends, for which they wrote their poetry on wooden chests, obituary notices, lemons, and other unusual materials.[2] The appearance of their manifesto in an influential journal under the thumb of 1980s-era poets triggered a substantive discussion.

The most significant and controversial manifesto was Ahmet Güntan's "Parçalı Ham" ("Fragmented and Crude," 2005).[3] There,

2. See poems by Kurtuluş and Efe Murad in this volume.

3. See poems by Güntan in this volume.

Güntan distanced himself from adjectives and rhyme. He stressed the importance of seeking poetry rather than creating it and announced that he would pursue a type of concrete experience not confined to the everyday. These were two of many manifestos published within just two years, proof of the liveliness of the poetry scene in this period.

Our map of 2000s poetry would be incomplete without mentioning the marked increase in the number of women poets during this period, including bold experimentalists such as Anita Sezgener, Aslı Serin, Fatma Nur Türk, Nilay Özer, Selcan Peksan, and Sevinç Çalhanoğlu.[4]

After the 1990s, discussions of Turkish literature centered around the novel. These discussions, which intensified after Orhan Pamuk won the Nobel Prize for Literature in 2006, also shaped debates on poetry. Nevertheless, the manifestos published in the 2000s and the central debate of this period demonstrate that poetry managed to return to its own agenda.

The Central Debate of the 2000s

The central debate of Turkish poetry in the 2000s pitted "lyric poetry" against "experimental poetry." The former preserved the language established in the 1980s, employing a poetics that was both imagist and narrative. The latter abandoned Second New's understanding of imagism, attempting instead to construct a new language. Journal articles and manifestos issued various criticisms and countercriticisms of these differences in poetic approach.

Curiously enough, adherents of both the lyric and experimental sides lay claim to the same poetic ancestors. If you ask poets of the 2000s who influenced them the most, they would agree on roughly the same names, including Atillâ İlhan, Cemal Süreya, Edip Cansever, İlhan Berk, İsmet Özel, Nâzım Hikmet, and Turgut Uyar. However, young poets emulated different qualities and techniques

4. See poems by Sezgener, Serin, Türk, and Peksan in this volume.

of these masters, so that even with a common starting point they arrived at entirely different destinations. Let us now examine the criticisms made on both sides.

Experimental poetry gained visibility in the early 2000s. Fragmented words, multiple meanings, various pursuits of form, and references to concrete poetry elicited strong reactions during this period dominated by lyric poetry. Experimental poetry, whose very naming had been the subject of heated debate, differed from lyric poetry most fundamentally on the issue of topic/object.[5] Many objects that lyric poets would never have regarded as a potential topic or ingredient entered poetry thanks to the experimentalists. For example, a crate of lemons or a proposal letter could be used as either a surface for writing or a poetic form.

Naturally, these developments led to criticisms about form. The most common charge leveled against young poets was that their experiments with poetic form had already been conducted years ago. Yet linking the legitimacy of an attempt at a new poetic discourse to originality is fallacious, for it completely brackets context from poetic history. Besides, if the yardstick for originality were form, then it would bear stressing that lyric poetry is not exactly new on the scene, either.

A parallel criticism deployed by proponents of lyric poetry was that by "reducing poetry to form," experimentalists prioritized form over content. This criticism betrays unfamiliarity with the history of aesthetics. Assuming such a rigid dichotomy between form and content trivializes the search for new forms. But we know from the history of not only Turkish poetry but also world poetry that, to put it

5. The terms used for the period's new poetic tendencies included *millennium poetry*, *neo-epic poetry*, *concrete poetry*, *visual poetry*, *remote poetry*, *two-thousandist new*, *surface poetry*, and *free work*. The common feature of all these different conceptualizations was the distance maintained from lyric poetry. Throughout this preface, I use *experimental poetry* as an umbrella term to refer to them all.

schematically, form is not independent of content and, indeed, often directly influences content.

The question of form does matter, but the real conflict is rooted elsewhere, and its scope is much larger. Experimental poetry elicited intense reactions because it challenged the very foundations of its opponent, reevaluating all poetic notions, not just language and form.

The various movements we have subsumed under "experimental poetry" shared the same aim: to *acknowledge and surpass* the language introduced by Second New.[6] This aim entailed doing away with imagism, but experimental poetry did not stop there; in many instances, it also completely abandoned conventional topics and narrative techniques. For example, Ömer Şişman's nine-page poem "Yerini Bulamayan Bir Z Raporu" ("A Z-Report Unable to Find Its Place") in *Bitkiben* (Plantself, 2010) expresses sociopolitical criticism without sloganeering, solely by listing all 720 possible permutations of a six-word news headline.[7] Such approaches, reminiscent of those used by French OULIPO writers in the 1960s, jettison the "reader-friendly" language discussed earlier.

In the early 2000s, experimental poetry received harsh critiques and rejection in mainstream journals on the grounds that it "isn't poetry." But those who previously criticized or disassociated themselves from it did come round to acknowledging its existence. Beyond proving its worth, experimental poetry, which was born as the critical wing of the poetry of the 2000s, has created its own discursive space.

Even though poets of various generations have established their own unique poetics, they exhibit, to use Wittgenstein's theorization, certain "family resemblances." These are based on a shared sense—extending all the way back to the technique of free verse—that the 1980s generation failed to grasp the narrative possibilities afforded by Second New's use of imagery. Though experimental poets follow different paths, they are "relatives" in the sense that they all

6. We can say that this aim was a form of *Aufhebung*, in the Hegelian sense.
7. See poems by Şişman in this volume.

fundamentally reject poetry's given possibilities, imagery-based language and agreed-upon forms, and seek instead new ways of conveying "experience." Indeed, the key to understanding post-2000 poetry lies in the concept of experience. These poets have criticized imagism for freezing and homogenizing experience. They have reached a new understanding of poetry by rebelling against tradition. To borrow Osman Konuk's apt description, they have "attacked the heart of the modern with something even more modern."[8]

In Turkey today, although those well versed in theory and poetics analyze and strive to historicize all that has been written from 2000 on, a growing number of young poets explore the connections among sound, music, and poetry through live performance, inspired by poets such as Ekin Metin Sozüpek and Emre Varışlı.[9] And inevitably, as elsewhere in the world, the latest discussions on experimental poetry address the relationships between poetry and digital assets such as NFTs (nonfungible tokens) as well as the potential effects of blockchain technology, artificial intelligence, and transhumanism on poetry.

Experimental poetry, which carved out a niche for itself by emerging victorious from the intellectual polemics of the 2000s, ought to acknowledge the contributions of avant-garde singularities. We cannot speak of an avant-garde tradition in the history of Turkish poetry, but such exceptional figures as Nâzım Hikmet (1902–63), Ercüment Behzad Lav (1903–84), and Asaf Halet Çelebi (1907–58) have burst onto the poetry scene with the brilliance of supernovas, developing new perspectives by defying prevailing norms. Their courageous isolated forays emboldened subsequent generations of poets to follow suit in championing the unorthodox. And so the avant-garde, despite its lack of historical continuity, has today finally achieved collectivism.

8. Mehmet Öztek, "Osman Konuk ile Söyleşi" (Interview with Osman Konuk), *heves*, no. 11 (July 2006): 29.

9. See poems by Sozüpek in this volume.

Translator's Preface

Buğra Giritlioğlu

The origins of this book date to my time in the Netherlands, some twenty years ago. Wallowing in isolation and self-pity as I then was, I set out to translate two favorite poems by Murathan Mungan about loneliness, never imagining they would one day appear in an anthology.

Over time, my trickle of literary translations, mostly prose, grew into a stream. It wasn't until 2015, when I met some of the poets featured in these pages, that I immersed myself in poetry and decided to edit an entire anthology of contemporary Turkish poems by living poets.[1] Within a few years, I had pored over 167 books and translated 215 poems. Of those, I have chosen 172 poems by sixty-one poets for this volume (see the appendix for bibliographical information about the original poems).

Many poets in Turkey today have grown weary of lyricism, of poems that resemble "poems." Their aversion to old-school lyric poetry led a growing number of them to identify as part of a so-called antilyric movement. This volume does contain examples of (neo)lyric poetry and many established poets, but it leans toward young emerging poets who tend to be more experimental.

Although most of the poets featured here have been anthologized in Turkish volumes, few have appeared in English translation. This

1. The contributing poets küçük İskender and Bülent Keçeli died before the completion of this project.

is due in part to the opacity of their work. Fortunately, because I restricted myself to living poets, they could help me disambiguate obscure lines. More importantly, translating previously untranslated work allowed me to share in the poets' thrill as the poems came to life in a fresh language.

I deliberately included emerging poets alongside the canonical, bringing together poets at all stages of their artistic journey. I sought diversity and balance in terms of style, technique, temperament, and outlook as well as gender, sexual orientation, and ethnicity. I also took care to represent poets belonging to different coteries, often segregated owing to rivalries and hostilities.

The length and organizational structure of this anthology changed many times as I wrestled with how best to present its poems. The story of its multiple incarnations and eventual publication could easily fill a separate preface. At one point, it even consisted of two separate volumes, with one organized by themes. I ultimately decided that any thematic categorization, no matter how witty or eloquent, would lessen the power of the individual poems. What Ayşegül Tözeren says about poets in her introduction applies equally well to poems: "Classifying poets . . . amounts to boxing them into little playgrounds—and that does not mesh with the free spirit of poetry." As such, I opted instead to organize them alphabetically by the poets' first names.

Nevertheless, this anthology remains loosely thematic because I mainly selected poems that ruminate on one or more universal themes of interest to me. Poetry is much more than a leisurely pastime. It's a matter of urgency, closely linked to survival. It's where we seek companions and answers to help quell our existential pain and panic. Here, I share my best personal discoveries.

Translating poetry presents many challenges associated with enjambment, wordplay, rhyme, rhythm, alliteration, and tone. Fidelity to all these elements is rarely possible. Luckily, poems often provide the opportunity to achieve the poet's desired effect—if not in the same spot as the original, then elsewhere in the poem. Complicating matters in the case of English and Turkish are grammatical differences that make it difficult to capture certain ambiguities of the Turkish verse.[2]

In instances where the poets used unusual wording, I opted to retain the deliberately peculiar rather than normalizing, explaining, or polishing. If any of the translations seem obscure, the reader can rest assured the originals are equally so. In a few instances, cultural subtleties came into play, which I have clarified in footnotes. I excluded poems that presuppose extensive knowledge of Turkish culture and history.

Many of the poems speak to each other. While some treat the anthology's themes in a serious, existential light, others address the same themes with humor. I hope the reader derives as much pleasure from these poems—lyrical, experimental, abstract, or concrete—as I have.

2. First, Turkish is a null-subject language; that is, sentences can lack an explicit subject, unlike English, which does require an explicit subject (though a subject *pronoun* is always encoded in verb conjugations in Turkish). Second, the Turkish third-person singular pronoun *o* can mean "he," "she," or "it." Third, for Turkish noun stems ending with a consonant, the possessive forms of the second- and third-person singular are indistinguishable in the accusative, dative, locative, and ablative cases. All three of these features are exemplified by the phrase "Sesini duydum," which can mean "I heard your/his/her/its voice." Add the more rigid word order of English into the mix, and it becomes clear why it is difficult to preserve the ambiguities of Turkish in English.

Guide to Turkish Pronunciation

Letter	*International Phonetic Alphabet (IPA) symbol*	*Description*	*Letter*	*International Phonetic Alphabet (IPA) symbol*	*Description*
A, a	/a/	as **a** in **far**	M, m	/m/	as **m** in **merry**
B, b	/b/	as **b** in **boy**	N, n	/n/	as **n** in **night**
C, c	/dʒ/	as **j** in **jury**	O, o	/o/	as **o** in **ore**
Ç, ç	/tʃ/	as **ch** in **child**	Ö, ö	/ø/	as **eu** in French **Dieu**
D, d	/d/	as **d** in **day**	P, p	/p/	as **p** in **pot**
E, e	/e/	as **e** in **stem** or **a** in **any**	R, r	/r/	as **r** in **ray** (a single flap)
F, f	/f/	as **f** in **fat**	S, s	/s/	as **s** in **sleep**
G, g	/g/	as **g** in **good**	Ş, ş	/ʃ/	as **sh** in **hush**
Ğ, ğ		"silent g," extends preceding vowel	T, t	/t/	as **t** in **tame**
H, h	/h/	as **h** in **hat**	U, u	/u/	as **oo** in **ooze** (but short)
I, ı	/ɯ/	"dotless i," similar to **e** in **system**	Ü, ü	/y/	as ü in German über (but short)
İ, i	/i/	"dotted i," as **ea** in **team** but short	V, v	/v/	as **v** in **victory**
J, j	/ʒ/	as **s** in **measure**	Y, y	/j/	as **y** in **yolk**
K, k	/k/	as **k** in **Kate**	Z, z	/z/	as **z** in **zebra**
L, l	/l/	as **l** in **list** (British accent)			

The Pulse of Contemporary Turkish

I, Creature

a small polite request on my part, this
the emptying of a plate, a glass's narrow escape from
breakage or the replacement of brains with
runny pantyhose,
(stripped of its prefix, few words are as asexual as hose)
this is as ordinary and simple a request
as the featherbrained sparrowhawks amid an imagined pink
grinning sky
and the convoluted surfaces confined to second meanings:
i want to be a creature, please don't understand me!

when for instance an octopus no longer in need of its arms
enmeshes in love-making turtles' pleasure juices before it can draw
breath
i want to be born. because i haven't been born yet
i too would desire a prehistoric body
and hooves
consisting of a belly laugh that flinches upon touching my shadow.
may my crimson height be remembered as the soothing of an
immensity.
and may now multiple heads fit into my untamed neck
my intent may be to cocoon—never expose—myself

because life doesn't exist
because pleasure is angular
because i embraced
a pleasant lie.

because right behind my internal organs is where my hands begin. i will use them well, i had promised everyone left and right. yet jaundice spreads, measles spreads. each of us is delivered into the same shit, on a different day. this is not questioned. i change shape, i change scope, i chain feeling. this is questioned. mornings play with their shorter-than-imagined tail. there are those who swear while urinating. there are those who swear while you're in, aiding. i restrain my arms, straining to slough off my shirt.

design me, i want to be a creature!

A. Emre Cengiz

Alpha 60

silence is complex, those who shed tears
and suicide. sometimes reality is possible in the present tense.
yet we're alone in the barrenness of possibilities. death and dot
s . . .* what about harmony, can it come in handy during the life
of the individual? words living in the capital of logic
must be freed from their regular orbits.† form:
possibilities' remnant wings
i'm somewhere far from tantalizing, the authorities
wouldn't understand that of course!‡

abundantly real-
ity or conscience. and anyway the better part of the future:
logical annihilation. when power's ongoing actions
consist solely of ignorance, time has no tears
day was in motion during the melting stage of legend
i walked into light: self-destruction!

"everything is a result
buy yourself popcorn and some oral communication!"

A. Emre Cengiz

* the dot is an orchestral silence, anyway! the essence of complex reality
† the night never gives up! and its ongoing curious actions
will tear down time's ever-extending weaves.
‡ the whole world is, you know, executed, as it advances in a straight line.

Stark

to all women molded by the starkness of pain

my shadow starts to breathe

i fall from my windmill onto the earth
inside me women and their eyes, women and their *hair*
moths wage a harmonious war in my naphthalene
my stomach conceals indigestible pure tortures
that's how i arrive at truth, my mind heavier than space, my name
beyond elephants

i'm frail, my voice fails to right itself on the planet stretched toward
infinity
i sew irresistible melodies to my skin
wintery space on my face, whenever i clash with my tongue
i swallow empty talk, a roadside in muş swallows humanity
and women bury the spring in their *hair*

i'm restless, my ears start to boil
my past smells of horse crossed with Lot
inside me women and their dreams, women and their love
beyond worn life, with the violence of flimsy time
i empty the blood in my lungs on white birds, may they fly

my shadow breathed long enough

Adem Göktaş

Orient Express

i'm my mother's longest night
the city, flowing across the window
like a diminished film frame
i shift with a cradleless pronoun
the orient express bends masculinity to a limping rhythm

i'm my mother's longest seventy thousand years
so far i can only count to one in my head
city one, train one, mother one, what about pronoun, is that one?
i don't know how to fold a child out of paper
yet all these years i've been mothering old paper

i've been my mother's coldest night for the last seventy thousand years
year summons year, road summons road, my lover summons my mother
we're still on the train, i wedge my head between platforms
mom, which car are you in?
pretty please pass by where the poem was written and follow me
i made a man of my lover, maybe i can make a man of the poem too

i'm my mother's longest night, my seventy-thousand-year-old poem
i don't know you darling, who are you?
introduce yourself to my mom, she knows everything
then throw yourself off the train
after all, one pronoun will replace another
my mother is the longest night in the poem, and i've missed the train

Adem Göktaş

Resurrection of Elephants

mankind has for years carried a crow's mind in his stomach

i glimpsed the infection forest from my wound
the troubles of djinns and gnomes allegedly in tree cavities
a dignified corpse whispered through soil's mouth:
there are poems due by resurrection
about the kinship between funerals and rapes

rancor becomes visible in the patter of the rain
interrupted by a good deed's thirst
scapegoats gather semen from ant nests
a mirror resurrecting elephants
battered childhoods
in a rhinoceros's mouth death smells just as you would fear

i watched your mind from the gate of my aches
songs of religions and of the deranged are in a pitiable poet's bed
a pained soothsayer explained before my birth:
there are books to be written by tomorrow
about liaisons between the lowborn and sleepless.

it was a sex-addicted god that endowed his sex organ to mankind

Adem Göktaş

Ring.

The feeling of goodwill rising in my throat
Returns as what I have taught people
And a manner of speaking.

I taught a manner of speaking

And unbroken things that keep expanding with repetitions.

Everyone knows that I didn't see any cacti in the desert:
This is a manner of speaking.

That a cactus doesn't signify anything else
Is a manner of speaking.

That a cactus in the desert is just a cactus in the desert
Is a manner of speaking.

Love differs from all this

And unbroken things that keep expanding with repetitions.

Ahmet Güntan

Crater.*

You wanted to tell your life story

To the sound reaching you as you stood

Before the crater.

You wanted to tell your life story to a black crater,
A black desert.
You saw what you saw before the crater and
Wanted to relate what you saw, before the crater.

Lava's transformation into a black desert
Where the ocean began,

When it transformed, when you saw it transform

You wanted to spread your arms, scream,

And disappear.

Ahmet Güntan

* This and the next poem are the section titled "From the Kilauea Crater."

Before the Crater.

Where we stand still and where we don't,

Before the crater.
Before the crater

As we keep going

Stop! Don't stop if you wish!
Make love! Don't make love if you wish!

Know, don't know!
Fear, don't fear!
Before the crater.

Before the crater

Know don't know, fear don't fear, make love don't make love,

The crater doesn't know, doesn't stop,
Doesn't fear, doesn't make love!

Ahmet Güntan

Opus Minimum

I realized too late.
I'm composed partly of what I don't want to contemplate.

Consider the similarity between İsmet Özel* and a Chinese man
They both talk a lot, if you listen a little it's enough.
Then again these are technical matters,
we ought to save the Chinese from this context.

The type of translating that scrapes itself is fallen on me
I realized too late. That there's no road once you arrive
Or that razing within hope is a type of raising

Long live the TOKİ† Republic. If I err I'll add another floor.
Atop my weariness.

I, now an accident report suited to myself
Found solace in this, I'm a bit slow.

Consider these excerpts from Beckett's *Murphy*
"*Would you like an Abundance of Imagery?*"
"*I shouldn't give you spattered words that go dead as soon as they sound.*"

* Turkish poet (b. 1944).

† TOKİ is the acronym for Toplu Konut İdaresi Başkanlığı (Mass Housing Development Administration in Turkey), which has overseen the construction of colossal apartment blocks across the country.

Spying on you through an ever-narrowing lens
Now referred to as fear of losing, this narrowing narrow we shall

They weighed death against parting
Parting came out fifty dirhems[‡] heavier
At the Karacaoğlan[§] juncture I'm sleepless still difficult

I realized too late again, you must have guessed.
I love you partly for what I don't know.

They left you a battered me.
Of course being me I realized it too late.

I'm a coincidence, beautified on colliding with myself maybe.

Ali Özgür Özkarcı

‡ An old unit of weight equal to about 3.207 grams.

§ The poet of the couplet in italics, Karacaoğlan, is a renowned Turkish folk poet who lived in the seventeenth century.

Why Was I Absent!? in 11 Questions (excerpts)

§5 *And are you a little romantic?*

Why was I absent, because I insisted on romanticism.
It was perceived as my tactic.
Showing resistance from both my tics and twitches.
To the wells of these buildings, the insolence of malls,
To this eye-porn century, these shop windows.
To your faces slipping into LED panels.
Like every other romantic I was my own spy.
Like every other romantic a *Selflancer.*
His clock broken, tick tock tick tock tick. Like. Tac. tic.
I broke myself with the cheapest of excuses.
I was present here. What's more, the most beautiful sell fee?
That is, he never mistook his conscience for a wound to be licked in his corner.
You got it. Just like it's pronounced. I was absent.

§11 *Eleventh question?*

Allow me to jab this question into myself.
And to fell myself, do allow me.
An occasional withdrawal into one's junkyard is well in order,
methinks.
It's mind-opening to upset the applecart of one's own mechanics.
I've been away from you all for a while now,
anyway, I'm sure I'll be back to reconstruct myself.

Ali Özgür Özkarcı

The Boy Who Hanged Himself

Everything weighed down on him
Words, lights, distances
His voice weighed down on him,
His glances in the mirror belonged to no one

The boy did not want to be foam
A flight suspended in midair
A pumice
Stung by water
He did not want to be an Oblivion
That parted into the petals of silence

The boy's weight rescued him one morning
From his shadow's weight
On the hour the pines ceased to smell
Beforeless, afterless

Alova

Death in Water

Every night the child would seek his stars
And the Moon, which he raised with brand-new names:
Cut nail, Luminous Hammock
Growwalker, Bruised Orange

When the wind would start blowing
Undulating the water's curtain
And a callow frog
Tire of its own croak
And jump into the moss-scented sky,
He'd lose his stars
The Moon he raised every night
Would shatter

When the wind subsided
So that the stars took their places
And the Full Moon recollected its pieces,
The child whose eyes grew heavy
Rested his head one night
Against his pillow made of the Milky Way
And laid down to the moss-scented stars'
Eternal sleep

Alova

Loveless Lovemaking

Faces slowly fading

Neither transparency nor ice

Only a hot salt
Scratching a glass mask
With its nails

The white skull of the desert
Awakens afar

Faces slowly vanish
In a shriek well

Vein cords envelop the room

Light tightens its nerve threads

Neither silence nor speech

Acid takes root in the rocks

Alova

*

Our left hand

Our surfacing childhood

Alova

n-39[*]

time[†] at the boundaries of words
inside sound ((you're inside the breast))
your voice is trembling. skin hindrance.
by saying "childhood is the seat of the skin."
those unable to mourn are in the corner
in doubt, so.
patience is for awaiting something
the dullness of infinitives, who knows,
a dragon committed affixless causelessness
felt cold on balconies, hard for us to say
a court document and a lustful house
a father on his semi-intelligent walk
you mistook that place for a breathless forest
you're inside the breast
and the harm is definitely not coming from you
exit, your "missing piece" exxxxx . . .

Anita Sezgener

[*] Each poem in Sezgener's book *normalia* (Nod, 2014), where this poem appears, bears a title that begins with an *n* for *normalia*, followed by a hyphen and a number. The book title is inspired by Foucault's aphorism "A 'normal person' is fiction."

[†] *Poet's note*: "Time is the measure of motion" (Aristotle).

Transparent Contours of Houses

corsets and hats. from a flickering glimmer. coal and sugar
reliefs. the Riga. of odds and ends. when with cloven glance
italicized.

the past shortens. on passing through the present
a meta-city. once Adorno said micrologic look.
as man's nature is to hurry about. he focuses on the smallest things.
if despite childhood's obstacles: illustrated books'
being written in sign language: pedagogy.
when transparent contours of houses are questioned. a trace. from
a child's first utterance. a hill tongue. smuggles silver from
nostalgia.

Anita Sezgener

Crows

what do you mean scare off the crows they're dying
on the grounds of the Muş sugar factory 200 crows die each week.
the authorities are investigating, so is the city's agricultural director.

they say the crows may have starved to death
the public doesn't believe this because the crows rummage through
the city's trash dump.
there are always some people lying always.

Anita Sezgener

Possibility

Scientists have failed to identify a definite cause for the pelican and
dolphin deaths along the Peruvian coast. although several fishermen
did all they could to resuscitate a few pelicans as they lay dying,
their efforts came to nothing.
experts posit the possibility that the cause of the mass deaths may
be a virus found in the animals.
again man is innocent.

Anita Sezgener

Why Is There?

you owe us a world

we need to make a fresh start
on a woman's gaze at a man
a woman's gaze at a woman
at herself, afresh
on an impossibility, possibility, belief
on opening the door, peepholes, closing the door
and ringing the bell, afresh

leaf and eve,
apple and adam
and forest and eve
and eve and eve

our transition from daisies to cactuses has certainly not been easy!

Aslı Serin

Such Is Life

don't be affected by seasonal rains.
the colors you see when you stare at the moon don't actually exist.
don't belittle the moment you said hey i'm still alive when the fish
in Azmak first touched your body as childishness.
all those who said they could warm your hands during winters;
are gone; don't be mad.
say this while looking at your hands . . . Say this to your hands.

don't get out of a car you get into to say yes
—at a moment when you decide you can change everything—
saying no because of the music that's on,
when you're stranded in the middle of the street
don't burst into laughter. Don't make decisions, say this
while looking at that music you said you wouldn't listen to anymore
at having said you wouldn't write anymore after your latest poem and
at your hair you just can't grow long
you, as a thing that can say, are so pretty.

you're now your own biggest consolation and consoler
suppose everyone else achieves their infinite order; let them
some people are tasked with achieving in this life
in new rooms and as the crowd grows and as the sounds grow
in the end a human being is actually a human being, don't blow
things out of proportion
this is partly why the places you are and you're not feel lonely.

so if there's a knife or a drill on the table for you
you can either wipe the dust off the table or bite it, it's up to you
don't meddle in that final bill to be paid though
because every story needs a happy.
"be happy, that's all that matters" is a bourgeois tradition
it's said with a smile that conceals the teeth.

evil can appear before you in different cloaks and guises
it can stand next to you, hang out with you
it may pretend to feint but never feint, it's thaddevil you see
is that where it hurts, there
with its magnificent sense of duty, there
as if all its life it'd been preparing for this moment, yep! right there . . .

look i will not repeat any of this:
stay away from those who explain things item by item and
those who've spent their lives ticking off lists
because you've never gone to the grocery store with a list
you saw for yourself, even pepper flowers first
the weather suddenly changes and it rains
the weather suddenly changes and the sun comes out.

hello, good morning, i'm Aslı, i learned the things i shouldn't be doing
from the things i did.

Aslı Serin

Maybe I'm Unavailable (excerpt)

you

it all happened while washing the dishes
owing to detergents that keep foaming and foaming
to my son's remark "my tears aren't like rain,
see, they're sticky"
to surfaces that show every speck of dirt
and to films that begin with "the end"
it was at the tip of my tongue
i was going to explain to you how to quit believing
this requires being incapable of flight even in dreams
this, sitting cross-legged and rocking
to the past to the future
to the past to the future
to the past to the future
no it's not a roly-poly

Aslı Serin

Script

maybe we were an impala
in the africa of wilting grass
how could you tell
unless you were a scavenger.

as the sounds blend into one another, *Dirmit*,*
and ravings stream from a comb
as that old old woman and girl whisper from the same mouth
we may be lost in the amulets attached to our childhoods
and in esoteric words; we may be deceived

with our grown self on a rooftop
under the pressure of the horizon's infiniteness
weary from lies incessantly told
we watch the world like a painting
as footsteps recede, our surroundings grow talkative
we two alone know this
we pick out the stones that have slipped into time
yet cannot divide time into bits

how can this tongue be translated into another
as the hum of conversation rises up the chimneys
without mystery words are destitute
may we die this time, we would say,
by thrashing against the glass of memory
our courage to murmur is a goat venturing on its trail

* Dirmit, a rebellious young girl, is the protagonist of the influential Turkish novelist Latife Tekin's (b. 1957) best-selling book *Sevgili Arsız Ölüm* (*Dear Shameless Death*) (Marion Boyars, 2001). The book follows her story from her early years in a small village to her traumatic move to the big city, bringing into focus the oppression borne by many girls and young women in modern Turkey.

we had first to pass through sound then word
those garrulous loquacious gabby trite words
no sooner did we lay eyes on the world than we wished our ears
would hear
when we hushed we didn't exist, chattiness was a requisite for
survival
we talked to flowing fountains, to early evenings
we flew from mouth to mouth and so grew up, spellbound

then we wound up in a dim library
found a mother in it
it does not befit a woman, they said, *Dirmit*,
books will chill you
aflame as we were with words
we did not say a thing
letters had hooks that glowed in the dark
it was the divine tablet, all blank
legible word for word
we were now script we were inscribed.

Asuman Susam

Enchanting

Music!
Is it waves
or the coincidence between the orderly arrangement of atoms and the arrangement of my atoms!
Is it the matching of halos! Is it the sharing of impossibility! It just is!
—Nilgün Marmara*

The earth seeks its root, shrinks to water
i'm toward a harmony-free music
atoms of sound follow in my tracks
the calm whiteness
that doesn't know whose dream captured it . . . i sink
i think with my hands now
my mind's worry amused by my body
skin's a big sentence!
you pay no heed to any of this

i eye ant nests, walk long
grasping every meaning, missing none
feels uncomfortable, this open intuition
i serenade before graves
to creatures underground
let sound rise to the sky, meaning sink to the bottom
the cave you enter may lead you to space
now wait, don't say what you have to say just yet

i touch my tongue to the cedar's bark
one should surrender to subthreshold perceptions
i hear with my tongue this erotic desire, flow of life fluid
enchanting sound
everyone knows it travels through corridors of silence
wearing away our visibility

*Nilgün Marmara was a Turkish poet (1958–87) profoundly influenced by the poetry of Sylvia Plath and, like Plath, committed suicide at a young age.

may a Stravinsky madness scatter, all askew
skip the din, bring on the whales
the fury of blue in our fissures running so high
pure time rescued from the hands of death
may you suffer defeat by a mournful wail alone
eternal loser, you're late to nature

white water; we're eye to eye, my eyes and i
our ravings and scratches multiply in silence
know but don't say: the secret's in the sound
it could make resistance visible
language falls short, but not a shriek!

Asuman Susam

Light

i believe in light
in the possibility of life and motion to last
i walk toward the Spanish broom
the mountain's yellow forehead
i've never encountered intimation in nature
but i do wonder about the love life of porcupines

the forest will soon flow as a flood from its slashed arms
blood clots will glow through the cracks in the bark
identifying whose sheddings leave it most lacking
i will go hug a silver birch
we will lose ourselves in the din of indivisibility
the shudder known as death
will grab me from my astonishment as i totter
it will puff up its feathers as it passes over us
we will believe in it, too, the way we believe in light

on reaching the mountain's airy balcony
we're lips that throb with pain after an intense kiss
this precipice doesn't make me dizzy, though:
i would grasp at my skirt as i fall, now and then soaring
falling is a way of descending too
roller coaster, wind corridor, repulsive force of matter
i, the law of inertia in the middle of the page
you'd better desert me wherever i may be

as love is a solitary wait
the thorn that forgets itself in the rose
sky that forgets itself in its cloud
i who forget myself in you
gallop, walk, trot, amble
all tried in times of departure

when light clears the way and metal separates from its burr
cuts will fill with memories, the valley with water

the saddlebag of the wait will hold oblivion
water will smell of a cloud; a cloud, of a forest
and my hands, of paper
light will shine for us to believe

Asuman Susam

A Leaf, a Stone's Leaf

as the waters began to darken
i saw with my sorrow heard with my desire
the light of the opposite shores

a leaf, a stone's leaf on that shore
kept dreams' aimless lunch bag for itself

like ants we were deep inside
our nest, joining shoreless
lost pieces with hungry lips
at the moist sound of the reeds

was it we who took turns bonding in this wound
or a world older even than its crust

it was knotted whites, gnarls, a scream
that immersed the back of ancient eras in a bottomless poison

as the waters begin to darken
i realize this cannot be the first darkness of this expanse
i neither die never to return
nor detach myself from him,

i part the lips of a shadow made of sun
i let unfought-for time flow
through wet leaves

Aylin Antmen

Your Blue Nakedness

there is no language outside of home, Ariel
like a fragile black forest
we shrink into ourselves mostly at night
and we withdraw into the sound of birds
when we have no courage left
to stare at that black sun
which grows no larger than a pupil

yet underwater your blue nakedness
loses its shadow made of death
loses sight of the atoms of dreams
strewn with sparks every which way

Aylin Antmen

I Fastened My Heart to Inky Roots

my life is a firestorm
i plucked my heart out of that storm
fastened it to inky roots

no stranger to being madly tossed
turning, as if desiring this moment's impassability
no stranger to being tossed and toppled
the soil of tongue's wings is wordless
how could i not know a nosedive
is a triumphant blood relation

my life, Ariel, my life is suddenly
an optical illusion
that grows night by night
by funneling the secret elixir of feelings
and that dreams of tempestuous rivers

i saw shadows drifting by, uninjured
dead glances gleaming in their sockets
i now trail the cold season
i, the most fearsome prey of pure reality
as the time-sun rises
on the surface of blood
so i trail
the wind left in me by god

it seems my loss is a red branch
fading fast from the memories of the forest,
i caught hold of it in its final moment
thousands of sparrows took flight from my chest
it was sound, blood, nearby
i never forgot it, Ariel
nor did i find solace

Aylin Antmen

Wilted Nature

Leaves, curled up and dried unto themselves
along the track
connecting a memory to a city,
do not heal.
Life recounts a futile journey
autumn amounts to calling at the wrong place
what rustles is the wind
leaves do not rustle.

Our eyes are like a long road
what comes and passes does not heal
in this night on this track
what is healed is time,
man does not heal.

Come, my life, trace yourself backward
there's nothing up ahead, you saw that
turn your face to the wind again
what is healed is not you, but time.

I flounder to remember a life
with my weak memory, clumsy perception
my life, o my life,
i extended my journey to remember you
allowed myself more time
in this night, in this midlife meadow
on this track
offer me a single word.

Birhan Keskin

Photograph

I am standing still in an old old photo.
Even there my face resembles an old photo.
A complex mythology, an intertwined tempo
stood to pose at that instant;
they still stand today.

A moment frozen in time in a huge blaze:
The foot of a bridge, except with no bridge,
standing in its place with sorrow.
A sunken fountain run dry
once for the public, and
a one-time smiling, then ruined old city.

Five women and a greenish sepia:
One sacrifices her life for the woman next to her,
In the third, a sorrow tilting her neck to the left
Remains just so. The fourth, a barely perceptible illusion.
On the fifth falls an ancient rain.

Apparently it was a black-and-white day,
in the depths of the photograph a silver stream,
and only it, flows out of the frozen moment.

Birhan Keskin

Pomegranate

We replenished the flowerpots with water,
and summer with memories,
under the grasshoppers' chatter and
the midday sun we waited
for the pomegranate to ripen.

We waited for the pain we suffered
in separate rooms to subside
and like a childhood dream
turn into a dull ache
we attached a pearly meaning to summer.

You know well
life goes on like vertigo,
summers attach alongside summers,
time turns into a long heat spell here,
into a feeling's burden and unbearability
and summers into memories . . .

Will the conversations we seek shelter in kill the pain?
Will the meaning of a tree's beauty not fade,
and love endure in its roots?
O my imaginary sister,
this love owes us;
let the pain we suffer in separate rooms subside,
the summer go by and the pomegranate ripen.

Birhan Keskin

Flamingo I

Even as it takes flight, a memory
slender and pink.
From one lake to another.

A sentence, so short, swift gait
no one to greet it.
Burns you so.

Then, left from me to you
Salt water and my thin
neck's memory,
hair-thin.

Birhan Keskin

Incarnation of Sound

he loved
humanity
so, but
silence even
more sometimes

so
he didn't mind
awaking before the others
and wandering alone

the köroğlu mountains

what luxury to wash up in a stream
yet as he strolled back up the hill
he felt his torso like a vase failing to find its flower

narrow, thin
supple yet solid
solid yet fragile
his ceramic neck tilted
stretched from his shoulder to his throat
vein by vein
fiber by fiber
lymph by lymph
clay against clay

the breath sprouting from the vase's mouth in place of a flower
couldn't cope with its nothingness, startled itself
became sound

indeed this vase's sole companion had all along been a mere mumble

the great spotted woodpecker too was first but a sound
he peck-peck-pecked from his hiding place
"what if the poet is unworthy?" he said coyly
"a poet worthy to portray me
has yet to be born . . ."
though eventually he succumbed, took a risk
was incarnated and
appeared

oh pecker of köroğlu
won't you perch on my bosom and peck me some too?
come peck this worthless body of mine
but, alas, what use is it even to you?

Buğra Giritlioğlu

Unborn Internal Organ Pain

for Professor Michael Cima,
in whose lab i used msb's
and whose sharp mind and sparkly eyes
once caused me great pain

if ever you've used a magnetic stir bar (msb) in labs
encounter one again
after a 20-year lapse
and it may
conjure up memories
drive you
magniacal
for the first time
stir a mind
not a liquid
cause you
unborn internal organ pain
twist your
insides
– aashy^{u}noo u w^{e}r sh^{u}post t^{a} b^{e}cum a grate sinetist –
it may, it may, it may

have you ever felt the pain of an unborn internal organ?

spinning round'n'round in its eddy
the nostalgic stir bar, 20 years saw it
transform into more than a metaphor:
no matter how much
you may have always likened it to
an ocean-thick heavy-deafy water layer steamrolling over us or
a tenacious fly that won't be chased away:
"look i'm passing, i've passed,"
time is now what rotates concretely
before you
piercing you inside
20 years, it turns (out), were razor sharp

spinning round'n'round 20 yearsyears
even when you're not watching
spinning-whirling. 20 × foreyears
all those msb's are a-spinnin'
the past 20 years they've been must've been, 20 exactly 20,
not even easily said let alone done!

likewise the multitek brand diaphone by your door. it flashes blue even when you're not home. blashes flue. day'n'night'n'day'n'night it. every second. when you're away on vacation for 1 week. for 2.5 months when you're.

flashOOON!ANDOOoff . . . flashOOON!ANDOOoff . . .

while msb's whirlworldwhirlworld every.one we die
flashON'n'OFF'n'whirl they be. alwaysss!!!

Buğra Giritlioğlu

Lukewarm Farewell to Lake Issyk

i'm packed, tent and all
the site was sandy
there alone
remain footprints

oh well. i'm unmoved.

i'll dip my hand one last time,
i kept on thinking since yesterday.
too bad i feel so indifferent this morning.
for the hell of it. through the motions. as a symbol.

i went and stood
before it
stooped down
waves ,_,_,
i sprang back
oh gosh my shoes!
might let in water
(supposedly watertight. the right is but the left's literally waterloose.
if it waterfalls it would watersink.)

not about brume and mourning,
rather broom and morning . . .
not even a poem this
with←in→difference.
i'd imagined
i'd be inspired, emotions running high.
no such luck

i dip my hand in
you
rub
my face

hope i don't catch an infection
feeling safe in your slight saltiness

what's that on my eyelid
my suture scar or sleep
felt it some more
not sure

like i said, this is definitely not a . . .
not(h)ing (in) difference

i see you're foggier today issyk wassup?
ever show the opposite shore clear as day?

my hands dried in minutes
some memory!

your pebbles a billiard ball each
their size struck me yesterday
thought let's write this! as i, my farewell done, was return-
billiard! only now as i was writ-,
brainwrack-
what kind of ball, what kind of ball
3ing

never about bru. .
                    or . . . me
differ . . . = 1 0 n e 1 y
only = 1 big ni 1

you're icy, not issyk* this time of year

Buğra Giritlioğlu

* "Warm" in Kyrgyz.

Stone Sink

if water doesn't run soap will bleed
on the spot and i
can't be buried into stone sinks

hidden in a faucet pipe
my eyes i can't see
in the rain that i drip

you Gods!
let every mirror i avoid
be inspired by you
and seek my face in the grave

Burak Acar

Sherotica

her mouth a hangar of fire
undress she says to the sky enter me

kiss my neck so she says
may my moles spread to your face

she says scorpions are ovulating inside me
they will mistake your sweat for rain

weary from cutting water with a saw
bathe she says in the black pepper lake
get out when i clap my hands
take off your shirt let it dry
hurry hang it on my nipples
with your teeth

i licked your back a scorching iron
it's after dark you must be hungry
she says my flesh is a dough of fire
knead me from myself
roll out borek on palace stairs

she says
they forced me off those blond horses
whose heads were buried in sun wells
come she says stark naked
from deserts of light

Burak Acar

A Daytime Sonata in Rome

to her

you're wearing a marble cape
your eyes, sea sparkle stirred up by the southerly wind
i spread the sky on our bread like this
i sat cross-legged above the chimes like this
carrying dried sun foam in his pockets
a child kissed our cheek in his brassy sleep
our soul, a tulle staircase ascending to the moon

from the fountains flowed candlelight
i presented you to myself like this
butterflies shrieked in unison like this
swans were flying in Villa Borghese
the black police horse at Popolo Square
was unaware of being a horse
we ate blackberry ice cream in Navona
were we two babies flying
from a smoldering forest to iced gardens
or water forgotten by gravity
flowing up a slope
were we drawings on the windows of paradise
red fish leaped from your eyes into mine
Michelangelo swept his brush on our lips

Burak Acar

A Bit of Fable / A Bit Lacking

to lorin

when the guide shed blood
the harbinger swelled: words
became history failed to document time
histories awaited time . . .

I

the black knot was tied around our heart.
when mystery protected our face as well.

the secrets on our skin find another face

II

                              in the facet of god
bandage to the manifold mystery dervishes . . .

the dream left on skin's mirror: healing
read: prayer

III

the body is our command. shadows seep from wells
our face is smooth in the cage

if a secret, the blind's word expands toward the tip
of a finger caressing keys to facilitate
passage through history consumed

IV

my past is a bit of fable: east
time unknown by history.

Bülent Keçeli

Psalms*

the desert began with dust this curiosity with innocence
the world, once roamed with revealed legends

curiosity striking tulle skins
sun stone shade
discovery that nullifies the face
tantamount to nothing but grandeur

codes climbing up from the soil to a tree
the unraveling we lean on issues its command
to the spirit of sound knot by knot (if a race)
skin's the fabric of our lovemaking

the soul i tailored for you transforms into strings
beads to the neck of our violence
curiosity warms to dreams through optical contacts
that rescue moans from precedents

i test dust to free myself from light
when darkness lets go, a feather
that rich voice a maqam in its new place

i knew again the radiant dream my thirst is broken
my hand's a leaf balance, its veins copper

* The original title, "mezmur'at," refers to psalms of the Zabur, the holy book of David. *Poet's note*: The title is an allusion to my fellow poet Murat [Üstübal]. Indeed, the whole poem is a tribute to our years-long friendship and many literary collaborations. [See two of Murat Üstübal's poems in this collection.]

he who bathes in dust becomes a line
coated with trouble as murmur
upsurge of pain in mad households
speed remains text 'urns to dust

speed; wave your hair's vibrant
having a laugh with its orange curls

to history: sea sparkle guise, totem intuition, heel
succeeded by dry eye or its buttons (open)

buttons are etiquette for my heart
its gate hollow'ness
its page suspect
from the poise on us scorpion collected by red

Bülent Keçeli

I Portrayed Myself by Hearing

in order to speak i had to forget what i'd heard
the interfering noise was the loveliest utterance
to call out to you i drew an upward slope
with a harmonica on a bicycle seat and
leaning my lines against the outlines of a bar stool
i waited for my voice to return from the audience
accompanied by a silence they came again from within

when i went outside my gaits also walked with bugs
as i the only one who trod in the pavement's footsteps
spoke i drew asphalts magmas, muddy
yet by the time i heard already a hand shutting the curtain on the couch
i have of course also been known to recline on the divan

those who recline on a divan yak away with abandon
words are in part forgotten as they're spoken
once i who listen to myself from my own portrait
rose from the divan i've occupied an armchair too
a silence accompanying me they came again from within

it was on that divan there that you last blew as long as a flower
and i always crossed my legs on a pavement across from your mouth
yet to portray my leg i also listened to your account of me
your breath filled my cheeks sounds are my skin's turban
a silence from within this portrait is a tongue-tied me

Cem Kurtuluş

Piss Sound Kids

piss sound kids
piss sound kids
writing's got a processless flow too
or piss sound kids pointing to the present
PISS SOUND KIDS!

Cem Kurtuluş

What Came out of a Bug

i dug and stole the bugs on me out of a mound
women, their laces bearing grass
i was a turbaned cavity, clenching earth
i undressed in the rain; earth, snotty kids
at the end of a balloon with ropes they wrapped
my hand in red sheets and collected it from my room

there were times i undressed into water with fear
kids in cavities, always covered in drool
the slug, unable to lift its foot off its ooze, i forgot their smell
and though i wanted to escape water as much as any bug
every hair strand i reached for grew with flowers rugs hamams
it was a cloud that drove the rain onto me
they watered the flowers in measured ways
every organ i internalized, a ballooning turban
they wrapped as they tugged and dug earth.

grass sprouts without suspending its gray tones
bugs scatter before seeing the rain
they swaddled me in scarves without undressing me
outstretched hands now emerge as balloon and rope

Cem Kurtuluş

DARK DEEP BREATH

TAKE A DEEP BREATH THERE'S SOMETHING THERE
SOMETHING THAT HAS WRAPPED OUR SPIRITS (OUR
BREATH) AROUND HORROR
AND HORROR AROUND OUR IN- AND EXHALINGS,
ALL INTERTWINED, MOVING HELICALLY IN AND OUT ↔
IN AND OUT
SAYING COME ON DEAR . . . THERE'S SOMETHING THERE
IN THE DARK
BOTH EYEING AND EVADING US
NEVER DUPED BY RUSES
YES I'M UTTERING THESE WORDS FACING DARKNESS
THAT DARKNESS RIGHT THERE, NOT THE
METAPHORICAL ONE
NO NOT THE BLIND'S, EVERYONE'S, THE ONE
STARTING FROM YOUR EYELIDS WHEN YOU SHUT THEM
THERE'S SOMETHING THERE
THAT HAS BEEN AWAITING YOU FOR A BILLION YEARS
TAKE A DEEP BREATH AS IF FILLING UP WITH HOLLOW
HUBRIS
LET THAT BREATH OUT LIKE HUMILITY LIKE A DERVISH
CHANTING AYWALLAH (H→) . . .
BE YOURSELF WHEN YOU BECOME YOURSELF
A DEEP BREATHHH, BUT TO WHAT EXTENT
CAN YOU BE YOURSELF ANYWAY . . . WE'RE NOT OUR
FACES
WE'RE NOT OUR FACES ASK DARKNESS
WE'RE NOT OUR SOULS EITHER, MIND YOU
"WE'RE ELSEWHERE" THERE IN DARKNESS
WHILE PEERING INTO THE DARK WE IMAGINE OURSELVES
TO BE A SPIRIT OF SORTS, THAT'S FEAR, JUST FEAR
THE BREATH YOU INHALE IS NOT
A NANOSECOND MORE PRECIOUS THAN ANYONE ELSE'S

WHEN YOU'RE GONE THIS PLACE WILL NOT BE LEFT
BREATHLESS
EVERY BREATH IS THE LAST BREATH THERE'S NO OTHER
BREATH
DEEP BREATH THE DEEPEST – THE BREATH OF FEAR
SUCKING IN WHOEVER SPEAKS WITH THE DARK
BREATH IS THE LETTER H SOUNDING WHILE MAKING
LOVE IN THE DARK
THERE'S SOMETHING LURKING IN LETTERS, IN THE
RESTS BETWEEN HEARTBEATS, IN THE DEEPEST
SHALLOWEST PLACES OF EXCHANGED AND EVADED
GLANCES
THE COURAGEOUS FEARFUL BREATH THAT HAS
SWALLOWED BOTH COURAGE AND THE FEAR INHERENT
IN COURAGE
SOMETHING LOADING CANCEROUS LUNGS WITH OXYGEN
THE HEART WITH ADRENALINE, CHOKING BOTH
NIGHT HAS FALLEN MORNING HAS BROKEN
OPEN THE WINDOW THERE'S SOMETHING THERE
TAKE A DEEP BREATH, BUT HOW DEEP
A BREATH CAN YOU TAKE ANYWAY
A BREATH IS DEEP INSOFAR AS IT LEAVES US BREATHLESS
TAKE A BREATH. THERE IS, NOTHING THERE.

Cem Uzungüneş

Exchanging Glances Evading Glances

to dear hermit Müjdat Sönmez

In spacious, reverberant waiting halls
loneliness casts cold, spying glances.
A dangerous story lurks in human eyes:
seagull squawks, ragged wine addicts,
doggedly flashing
dank lighthouses of the wait.

Wet, melancholy cats pass by there
tightly clinging to their ash colors.
There, in that gray, sorrowful railway terminal outside time
on the long platforms of our unease,

as tepid cat paws treading on wet marble steps
shake out water, so may we avert our eyes
from the shallow, rinsed gaze
of women with raincoats, men with umbrellas,
as r e f l e x i v e l y;
worrying that our eyes may (not) meet
may we and a very old (near-dead) acquaintance
avert our eyes from each other with a chain haste
as if playing old maid with our glances
so our deepest unequivocal loneliness
does not get stuck in our dealt hand.

Growing estranged from the present tense
in waiting halls with frozen clocks,
exchanging glances with honey-colored, glowing cat's eyes
which in Baudelair's view bespeak infinity,

until the train storms off
from the long platforms of our unease;
evading eyes until every hesitation dissolves,
on a final trip to the home of desire (oneself)
until the train storms off,
toward a familiar but far, faraway, near-dead
time town.

Cem Uzungüneş

Scorpion

Surrender yourself to the scorpion
advancing between your breasts
toward your groin my love,
surrender yourself to this cancer's metastasis,
to your soul's shrieks.

This forbidden love
is a question mark inside you
resembling that scorpion's alarmed knotted tail
standing between you and your breath
you and the world.

Carry it carry that scorpion inside you.

Surrender yourself to your soul's venomous orgasm.

Cem Uzungüneş

Women Perform Ablutions with Joy

"I'm Ashamed of Fiqh"

we smell nothing like blood
the keyboard doesn't smell of blood either
nor do banana peels or cell phones
the prime minister's advisers
a cigarette butt freshly ground into an ashtray
the south of istanbul and experimental ox
don't smell like blood
we cannot smell the sound or color of blood
but blood would want to be smelled too
i personally don't think
blood enjoys being drunk or observed
surely a bona fide blood,
even if it's a feminist, would want to be smelled

i need a new color
i'm bored of red
of circulating inside you and not smelling
of not being smelled
of bandages and feminine pads
of the force exerted on me by the pressure outside
of the monitors you suck light from with eyes
no one has ever seen a monitor
bleeding or smelling when it breaks

but going back to me

slowly and sadly
i drip from a nose

a woman
performs ablutions
joy'fully

Cihat Duman

An Angel Outage to Remember

if your shoulder
does not bear the footprints of a butterfly
fallen shortly after taking flight
it's bound to have ties with those in power
not to be kissed

you live beneath the angel
who recognizes me from my lips
you've been embraced
even your kidneys seem so beautiful
not to be kissed

therefore spiders proceed in the direction
when viewed at shoulder height
extracted with hard eye consonants
from their eggs to cry and thus
not to be kissed

Cihat Duman

Entirely Letter

these here are my hands turned toward birds
real birds
come kiss me already i'm about to cry
come forgive me i promise it won't hurt
that phone can be switched off
that world can get the hell out of the roaming area
i can whistle for your ears
i can love you very much
let's pass by a butcher shop together
then i can love you very much then
we can take a shower

these here are my hands it's snowing
you must have a plan for my hands
come kiss me already come bleep me
let's pass by a butcher shop together
let it not last till the morning
or let me scream stark naked at the window
  — O those who've had their right to go crazy snatched by the
                                                                government
  you're the nicest people on earth

i can also tell you briefly how a rose explodes
that there can be no such thing as literary art
  like *istanbul is just so beautiful this letter is so beautiful*

your slap and orange peels
from the most genuine side of democracy
come to me a while i beg you Put on my sweater

Cihat Duman

Relationship. .[*]

. . . Interesting. . it ended up collapsing where it was born. it fell right where that instantly fearful, bashful twitch on his face got caught by my eye and remained in my eye, and where his gaze, not directed at anyone present, shaken by instinct, was ingrained in my memory. the puzzle and dazzle are settling . . . ashes with dying sparks are flying about, landing all over me . . .

. . . From now on only and again and ever: he will stumble and fall from the slopes he's treading in a daze. also, i will trip him up into my dreams—as an act of violence.

The seagulls, banished from their heaven, flocking around the city's rooftops and garbage dumps, are not about to let anyone relish this sticky sultry Istanbul night. No one may free himself from their squawky whining and wild yells and take refuge in this night or personalize it!

Let all those who remain in the night either adjust everything to this unrelenting seagull perversion or be excluded from this night! . . .

Who knows what provoked them now? Perhaps the sparks flying from the death throes sprawled out between him and me, an entrenched lament? entreaty? curse? for the dead Marmara they have lost. . or fireworks going off at nearby turkish celebrations. . why should i care, why should anyone care—but those brazen seagulls dive nonstop in and out of this piece of time that's become a veritable sieve.

A gleaming half-moon in the sky holds on to then lets go of the shredded clouds drifting by, bats make a dive above my head, my

[*] The use of two periods is becoming increasingly prevalent in Turkish literature. Poets cite various reasons for using them. Some say they prefer them to ellipses when they want a shorter pause, while others favor them because they find the ellipsis too old-fashioned and clichéd.

female and male dogs tremble besides me, both on edge, awaiting the weasels soon to descend from higher gardens to hunt. Whether the clamor that erupts comes from the weasels' fascination with their prey or from the strangled mice, it is hard to say; in any event, it is the sound of a quick execution. .

An unexpected inauspicious wind blew, rustling the leaves, "morning!" I thought to myself, and the half-moon, like a pale rag, slid toward the corner of the sky, light appeared. The last bat of the night circled above me, revolving its blind and deaf body, captured by daylight, with the haste of its velvety wings, making me shudder, and finally vanished into the dimness. The call to prayer sounded from afar, the howl of dogs. . when the boisterous chatter of the sparrows was added to the never-ending seagull insolence, all unsleeping beings knew an irreversible thing, the day, was dawning.

Now: with papers or ashes?

Defne Sandalcı

On the Lookout in the Courtyard (excerpt)

1c- ca ce cı cae

also, i was a water creature, i recall, close to land, the line where water met land was at my eye level and water would flow, and on land were a house, road, and tree. The house appeared as if it had just left the water and perched on its shore. I would watch from the water. . . .

(take water's heart,
make a list of water places)

1d- de du da dun

From the garden I escaped inside, back "home."

PRIMARY ISSUES. MEMORIZATION OF BODILY BOUNDARIES, INNER BODY, MAP OF NERVES AND NERVE ENDINGS, RESPECTFUL AND DISTANT (intuitive and clinical) RELATIONSHIPS WITH INTERNAL ORGANS, STRATEGIES FOR WITHHOLDING OBSCENE BLOOD, AESTHETIC ADJUSTMENT AND TOLERANCE—LIFE WITH OUTER WOMANTHING BODY. METHODS OF EXITING HOME, VIRTUES OF BREAKING AWAY FROM HOME.

(make a list of nerve endings snapped during riot accidents.)

TACTICS OF OPENING UP INSIDES:

Don't lie on your side. Don't lie down at all. Use eyes, heart, hands, and feet. Use nights. Hide during days. Wear the shells of insides to be filled.

(list emptied insides)
(inventory miracles)
(gut whatever prevents you from dying)

Defne Sandalcı

Inside an Experience

whetted words leap out of the curtain
nascent fires carve an identity into marble
hands are flighty, people ravel-mouthed
but raw wrath spills over into the universe
so let's find ourselves in another

a persistent solitude on the painter's palette
remove the stains so the clouds ascend
let blunders fall from our story
let all those memorized details be defaced on lips
whoever steals his fabric from pain is experienced in another

let us preserve this instant in the wrinkle of the night
let the face i lost in play not be roughed up
let iron toughen, steel harden
blurred men may depart from me
and the maestro eyeing the ney may polish my cough

a weary brush strokes your child face
the bullet of that sought-after death is found

Duygu Kankaytsın

Sea Now

as your skin swelled against mine
on a daisy morning
the eventual fracture of a mountain
was the face of soil

feelings are defeated, the lancet rusty
entering the river, a fugitive
sharpening human scent, isthmus
of uterus rinsed, the pain of words in her mouth

love creates but a water sac
the sound of our ever-swirling river
a woman on her own shore, alone
as you step into the sea

Duygu Kankaytsın

Dream's Demise

it was white, it was black; it was later
living so was at the tips of pins and needles.

when Nietzsche kills god
the city like a wounded crocodile
a lash in the hands of the mob
a lizard of fire on the woman's face
shadows pass above her
flesh-eating ants on her skin
in her palm, the world, vanishing as she squeezes it
the sky tearing as she pulls at it
the plane tree sinking into her belly
the sea drowning in her lungs

your hands never had a history
but if you need a witness ask wheat
and stones, and the love that warms water.

time is a growing monster
its morning is wild, another of its days about to be stolen
darkness will greet it after work
the window it reaches for, blinded
its dog thrown onto the street
killed once more is
the dream she hides in her wooden chest

Duygu Kankaytsın

Raw Light*

i had a big love affair at sixteen
i opened my whole heart, we separated
then i had to close that heart back up
i didn't manage to do that and i encountered poetry
but i didn't know i was going to write any, i was just reading poems.
one night i woke up, at three in the morning, i went
and opened the fridge, i was getting something
i was gonna drink water or something, it was pitch-black
it wasn't like houses today, you didn't turn on the light.
there used to be a central space in houses back then
since the hearth was there, all the rooms opened up to it,
you couldn't turn on the light and go, so when i opened its door
suddenly a light shone from the fridge
i stopped, i felt something in that moment.

Efe Murad

* *Poet's footnote*: This is from the sound recordings I made secretly during my conversations with Ahmet [Güntan]. Ahmet was talking about his first exposure to poetry; a different version of this story was apparently published as part of a discussion with Ömer [Aygün] in the eighteenth issue of *heves*. As my friend Doğan Hayyam put it, the "fridge Buddha" revealed itself to Ahmet. [See poems by Ahmet Güntan and Ömer Aygün in this collection.]

Nabataean Script

all alone in the desert with a Jeep
i can't find anything to write about in the desert
you shout the sound doesn't go anywhere
you're left with the act of shouting
there's no echo, you're just shouting at the sound
the sound leaves you
and sinks into sound

this poem was written in the desert beneath the stars

Efe Murad

You're as Much as a Desert

scriptures are made up by people.
i was abducted by lonely people in the desert
nothing, simply nothing, what more do you expect
having once tasted infinity, Deadsea the Ripper!
it doesn't befit you to have forgotten how to live,
the doors you leaned on shut of their own accord
into walls, let the killing permeate, my white body
reaching for your flesh, my skin indulges itself.
momentlessness fills you, knowing to die when it's time
as stars, feigning denial of beauty, transform
spontaneously in the reflection of space and time
you are my dark moments, Deadsea the Ripper!
petrified into salt, you remain just so at rock bottom
as if you discovered where revelation descended,
space day, as much as a desert
when you're duped all alone and find your own place
you start to believe everything has a creator.

Efe Murad

A Raving Dyslexia (excerpt)

"for man is neither animal nor god"

Digital Art Tower
Dragged down an overhead projector, the subjects are duly debased.
My ivories are broken. As a single-toothed monster
I'm spreading my forgiveness from top to bottom
I'm shooting society's lynx, society's lion
With my organic weapons spying on society's wild life
from this digital art tower
they're gutters of self-sacrifice I belittle by wordicizing
I'm a deity to them. I have a green fedora
I have a green fedora and in the projection my hesitation
tangibilizes as big as a skyscraper,
in the momentary reflection whose sparkles pulverize the eyes.
Withered with art
withered with Art
Let your beard Down
slow down and
begin to be able to assemble;
with a stubbornness inspermiating
their televisions to the emergency exits of warethics
with a stubbornness leveling
magazine bulletins to uniquality for all
(make them jump rope) until they're equalized under zero size
in response to their bestiality, letsee an outfit in jealousy
kill them by clothing/undressing them
Code the Modes / (mode-evaded by) independent and unbridled
Fashion

Welp our gunpowder, feign willpower
we never tire of deities who bloody us
laugh as if you've never inhaled from your flanks never been shot
carry on, feigning willpower, pushed like a slave from pillar to post
Why don't you (re)move the capital letter from the beginning
to the end of the linear time constrictly imposed on you.
    spirals oval chatter regions fractals that cannot contain curses
fractals
    that impose the explosion and disperse the atmosphere and gas
    ruledenier adagencies that scatter your insides by spinning rip
                                                                                    you off
    and let a puppeteer format their shy individuals.
your XYZego
strewn by scholarlycopywriters of ad agencies
sharing the fee for the brilight ad you incorporate into your brain
to beautify your identity
                              with thebureaucrats,   agencies
                              whose agents are those?

Ekin Metin Sozüpek

Enemy

the
the (little)
the (little) (boy)
the (little) (boy) (looked at)
the (little) (boy) (looked at) (his dad) (and)
said:
p
pa
pap
papa
papa s
papa se
papa see
that
that girl
that girl's peepee
that girl's gogot no peepeepee!
when
he saw his son
stutter the father
laughed (and at his courage).
so-
son
all tense
asked again:
papa
why
dushshe
hahave nono peepee?

his dad:
did
you look
under
her dress
where
did you
see that?
papa,
she came and
showed it
to me
herself
Where?
There!

—he pointed to a rose garden fenced off by barbed wire.

exuding an air of imagined departure
someone who had just bitted his horse was feverishly digging the soil
as if with seeds in hand

Ekin Metin Sozüpek

Abandoning a Name

Mirrors choose you
Your laughter is the howl of narrow passages
I split your voice into matchless pieces
Your face landed far away
Your eyes sighted in passing ships

The water in the old well
did not stir when you left
Tears did not flow
The song of the gardens did not stop
The sky remained in place

I too can depart if I wish
The road would end on my departure
I would become a sketchy figure
Her traces dark
Her darkness menacing

I slice nights with the thinnest moon
A pain with steel teeth gnaws at my mind
Only unnamed children would understand
I have long abandoned my name

Elif Sofya

Melek Angel[*]

to Melek İrez

With the curse of girls
Flung from Bursa to Halep and dipped into blood
The needle forged of breathless iron
Quivers in the whiteness of lace magnifying her hands
I see clamor in your chest
Animals with wounded mouths in your shadow

The dead train crushing your youth has tousled your hair
Stretched between the expulsion and now
Even if one by one I gather every strand
At whose tip a smiling fox speaks
Are your troubles prolonged
With longevity Angel

This fabricated history that named you Melek
Persists and permeates my open wounds
The reason I left my childhood on your lap

Elif Sofya

[*] "Melek" is a woman's name in Turkish, meaning "angel."

Boomerang

Let me blow mustard seeds your way
Send you the plash of water
Ululating and uniting from earth to sky
A boomerang in my mouth

Let us not know
How to pick the right thorn for our flesh
And assume an elderly manner
Or anything else
Let us gird on speed and fly away
A no one to anyone
Then
Nature would become natural

Elif Sofya

Sema* of the Lake

The lake, a subtle ache in the reeds neyZen†
And the Francolin calls out to me: Linnn . . .
As the francolin whirled, the lake spilled
Off her feathers reflect and silver and the moon
The lake went "puff"

The francolin moaned, her heart wrung in the reeds
Listening to the ney on the lake's breath
She stopped and bowed toward the slothful lake
The moon broke, silver spilled, and to my skirt,
Unfolding with choked pleasure,
Said the lake as it whirled the sema: Francolin . . . Francolin . . .
Francolin . . .

And there, LOVE SENSED all my moods

Emel İrtem

* The whirling dance ritual of the Mevlevi Sufi order.

† A ney flute player.

Period

a scolded rose in a vase, Summer
its posture thinned from conceit
perhaps skimming the lady's countenance,
summer, replete with horses and butterflies,
would vaporize, effaced from the rose
summer remains in my winter nip, Rosesetter

i say. Or the season's leaves
the lady would shed
during curtainless summers she longs for autumns
as if she's fashioned a rose from her reflection
she eats rock crystals whenever she hungers, Stonesetter

i say. Roses sour in the lady's hair
summer, suffused with the smells of pilaki* and cinnamon,
begins to burn and turn to ash
the lady is a pastoral love anyway
her young womanhood bleeds in old photos
the past often recurs, Poemsetter
i say.

yesterday the lady kissed me
she split her bosom, spilt it from the vase
i say blood/period
she says Commasetter and bows in shame.

Emel İrtem

* A type of meze, cooked in a sauce containing onion, garlic, carrot, potato, tomato, and olive oil.

Waltz Triste

it is said that yellow and purple things sometimes come together.
the day i saw you for instance was yellow, i swear. two pelicans
were pushing a tulle skiff with waltzing steps, i swear on that
too. i swear on some holy books and of course by touching my
tongue on a leap. the other day i swore on a scratch realized
for the fairy tales i told, on cold-soring daydreaming, and on a strip
of bandage. because these are incredible things. incredible and purple.
you can't prove it. true, i can't prove the waltz triste playing in
the background right now, either. because some purple things
come only to disappear, i swear on the carbon monoxide
coursing in my veins.

Emel Kaya

70° Memories Cologne

was that really spoken now in the narrow corridor
while drinking tea or shaking out horns
the hand clutching the glass is an acorn
a single letter's length: perfume, water, tobacco, cologne

i am a shadow of myself, a spirit kicks up dust in me
linen background, display windows, TV stand
sob more come on shake out those horns

pour me into my body, it foamed and spilled to the ground
pour me into my body, there my shin bone, my soft tissue
ripples expanding in my barely living daylights, a tar lake rising soft
and bare

save the deer
drown me
sob sniff sputter shake out those horns

Emel Kaya

Introduction to Mercury

i've heard many stories about mercury
a mouthful of mercury
to die of laughter from mercury
a heart of mercury
—do not inhale its vapor!—
a kidney an odd clot
the face thrown into a toilet bowl
and the pressure splattering from the finger
segment flushing that toilet
rituals of thanksgiving
the hand hanging from a shoulder
a terrible faux pas
return and additional services
are all from mercury

whistling happily
is not

Emel Kaya

Lacking-II

man's neck is clogged
his living is clogged congested
choppy is man's voice
his clothes either too short or too long
man is bizarre

man struggles
he experiences and watches his own failure
and that of the dying world, of every damn thing
there *is* such a thing as struggling

and man dies
this is so real and absurd

poor man

Emrah Altınok

Lacking-VI

man desired woman
desired her so
as her shell was peeled
in man's nails

man undressed woman
an acidic spray scattered into the sky
swallowed laid on beds
thus softened houses

but in vain
in vain is lovemaking
inscribed on the earthen slab
woman and man
shall not make a whole

Emrah Altınok

Foramina Patent*

lumbar lordosis mildly flattened
in upper lumbar region
disk signal intensities
and heights normal
vertebra corpus heights unremarkable
no osteodestruction-related
signal changes

minimal increase in convexity
noted in L5-S1 disk
no clear evidence of epidural compression
canal diameters unremarkable
foramina patent

a small disk protrusion
with left paramedian localization noted
at T12-L1 level
lesion pressing minimally
on ventral face of dural sac
canal diameters unremarkable
foramina patent

distal cord and conus medullaris unremarkable
conus localization normal
at other levels intervertebral disks
and intracanal formations unremarkable
canal diameters normal
foramina patent

Emrah Altınok

* *Poet's note*: A lumbar spine MRI report excerpted exactly as is. The poetry in the report recognized by S.

Hell Refers to the Place Where the Offended Assemble

my ten-year-old self with huge eyes asks:
i get that my dad's dead
but why doesn't he come home in the evening?
when he doesn't come, the salad's always left over

Enis Akın

Petty Tiffs of Imperfect People

that's right honey i'm a good-for-nothing
even more than you realize when you say that
with my sins, my false promises,
my habit of picking my nose, my sockless feet
this kid
will wake up early one morning
to take revenge on those who let him be crushed

all in all
watching your questions turn pathetic one by one
how you don' luv me right?
the excuse is like, this life, this you, this curled
smile of yours and this waiting to penetrate
and since
we made love with fire we played
vengeance is fun, honey, who knew
and the fulfilled life, neat-wardrobes life
only-the-bud-of-the-onion-on-the-table life
that i suggested naively out of the blue
were all wrong
instead, watching you watch me tremble
like a local ferry approaching the dock
in a morning aria
boooooooooooooo
was it humility to wait for your hips to grow
one by one
you're about to yell
but yelling doesn't solve anything
bury your head into the pillow

since
i failed to be that man who never stops inspiring hope
from now on *i* will inhale every cigarette you smoke,
into my lungs, hon

Enis Akın

It's Not Like We Were Goin'anywhere Even If We Didn't Get Caught in a Current

eversince plato invented love
my doctor and i are painting scarlet
my life which burned
in a computer crash

bottle openers no longer open beers or anything
the only functionin' utensils left in the house are lighters
lighter: first to be rescued from a fire, i'd say

as i pass through the smoke
it passes through me

i've begun to worship fire

in my bedroom an active volcano
and a needless sense of justice

the smokiest of these fires
broke out in an arson
with my doctor i'm painting red

my glances which ignite and burn like leaves
eversince plato invented love
every night i cover my face with my hands
and kiss satan's hands

Enis Akın

Wealth

"Wealth is like glass," says Syrus: "It shines
but breaks." If I write on glass or a mirror it smashes to bits,
if I write on paper or wood flames engulf it,
I wrote on stone: Tempestuous winds effaced it.
My poetry is my wealth: Written on the sun it will die out
one day, written on the night between the stars
a period, comma, question mark: Darkness is like glass,
it shines and breaks, says a dark voice inside my head—
all I have left is a hush: My petrified alphabet.

Enis Batur

Etna

The lava inside Etna is bubbling up.
Every day every unit of tremor is kept under
close watch in the lab at the mountain's foot.
Experts observe with regular reports
the sleep of the silent magma extending from
the crater into the depths, stirtectors are taking
its pulse with strange hiccuplike sounds.
Philologists still seek the author of the didactic
poem of sixhundredfortyfive hexameters.
It's almost certain Vergilius did not write
this poem. So is the fact that
the mountain sleeps on toward
night's end: A step stands,
all empty, between two doubts.

Enis Batur

Albino

I lost count of the nights and days;
I was an untamable shell above
the snow-white sea, a blind stain tossed about
by long albino waves so high they touched
the vault of heaven: Weary, my fear
long abandoned, I waited, at once an infinite bird
hovering between two apathies
and a breathless beast of the dark
at the bottom of a well, not knowing
how many nights and days had elapsed,
having long renounced myself,
there were moments when I cocooned,
withdrawing into the distance,
had the axis through me broken,
had the bow steadying my body stirred
from its roots, i couldn't tell:
how many mornings did the sun
not rise, on a black day following
the deluge sent to me, i awoke.

Enis Batur

TURGUT UYAR TRILOGY*

I. Turgut Uyar Confessional

kvetchkvetch
kvetchkvetch
kvetchkvetch

kvetchkvetch kvetchkvetch kvetchkvetch
kvetchkvetch kvetchkvetch kvetchkvetch

kvetchkvetchevk
kvetchkvetchevk
          kvetchkvetch
kvetchkvetchevk
kvetchkvetchevk
          kvetchkvetch

kvetchkvetchevk
kvetchkvetchevk
          kvetchkvetch
kvetchkvetchevk
kvetchkvetchevk
          kvetchkvetch

kvetchkvetchevk kvetchkvetchevk kvetchkvetchevk
kvetchkvetchevk kvetchkvetchevk kvetchkvetchevk

kvetchkvetch
kvetchkvetch
kvetchkvetch

* A highly acclaimed and influential poet, Turgut Uyar (1927–85) was among the pioneers of the so-called *İkinci Yeni* (Second New) movement.

II. Upward-Leaning Front-Sight Error†

three tımes three equals nıne
697 ıh92
5y3 w17q43 9r 9h3 ğw 9h3
w9 ğw ğ5w w17q43 4995
697 ıh92
[5y343'w h9 w7dy 5yğht qw yq006 o9f3[
697 ıh92

g75 w54qht3o6 3h97ty
ğh w04ğht 94 975wğe3
7he34 5y3 ğhrğhğ53 wı6
o9f3 5ğj3w o9f3
qo2q6w 317qow ğhrğhğ56
r94 w9j3 43qw9h

and ıt has no square root

† Ergun Tavlan applied a coding scheme to Turgut Uyar's poem "Sibernetik" (Cybernetic) to derive this section of his poem. The translators applied the same code to their English translation of "Sibernetik."

III. Gestalt

three tmies three qeuals nien
you konw
the sqarue of oen is oen
so is its sqarue roto
you konw
"three's no scuh tinhg as hpapy lvoe"
you konw

but straengly eunogh
in spirng or otuside
unedr the inifnite sky
lvoe tiems lvoe
alawys euqals
ifninity
for smoe roeasn

adn it has no sqarue roto

Ergun Tavlan

Decibel Settings

amble siren (two decibels
the straw that broke (three

slogan shouts (four decibels
police outs (five

calls to prayer (
trays (
riend whistles (

music in the teagarden (two decibels
taverna (one

whatever's in my techno
life's a summary of all that
politics in the goalpost

fullback foursome a de facto poem
all four some poem!

chest in midefiled

if having traversed all these sounds i arrive home
having transcribed all these sounds

place them before you right here

what would you imagine i did
i silenced sounds

you'd imagine because this is a thinkment
Ursula must have washed you

speaking is an event (one decibel
i write (two

just not true sounds do exist
they form a parliament

i grant them immunity
my writing is a thinkment

sign language at center forward

Ergun Tavlan

Inner Self

fissures
open in his mind
effacing any tender feeling
from his face

rootless
                aimless
                                keyless
                                                ill-tempered

in the depths
so many torn ends-of-the-day
on the surface
exitless beings
                                embracing flames
kiss fire
                        make love to fire

the inner self buries its skeletons

Erkan Karakiraz

Steps

zigzags
on the needle pine
shaken by the wind
the penchant for grass
of the cat
with a stomach ache
paw prints on ash
an established communication-gap mechanism

yet
all that comes
to pass in life
spills semen
on the opposite shore

a long
wounding
slope
life's steps

soundproof
interior unseen
falls
into existence—*a dry p sound alone*
softly touches the soul

Erkan Karakiraz

Assumption 3

march tenth, 11:10:04 pm

what you ripped out, what hid behind lungs
is not a heart; but its mask
merely: gilded, sparkly, kaleidoscopic . . .
the reflection in my blood
of your love which has wholly permeated my corporeality. the soul has become superfluous

Erkan Karakiraz

Shedding (excerpts)*

(p. 11)

you await a miracle: from yourself and everything else: coming here was the miracle: giving birth to time: as time functions perfectly your body malfunctions: you have no name only a pulse: if you exist you can see countless possibilities in all that comes to pass outside of you: while visible you're outside yourself: while invisible inside: the only thing you will see is that your body hardens by the day: it is not the person that hardens but reality: possibility vanishes: as long as the body sheds blood: possibility is in your body: as long as blood flows through your body: a tree without a shoot is illuminated: the sun is striking: the world crosses into silence like a baby embracing sleep: something will happen you will forget: nothing will happen you will never forget—

* These excerpts appear on the pages indicated, in the book *Döküntü: Bir Şiirin Can'ı için Kantat* (Shedding: Cantata for the Soul of a Poem) (Yapı Kredi [YKY], 2016). The poet regards the entire book as one single prose poem.

(p. 12)

a woman will pass by: you will look at her face: as you look at her face you will avert your eyes: you will return to the blank page and scrawl words that match a face. you will dismiss what you wrote as twaddle. you will bury them all in their scrawled disquiet inside emptiness: words will not blink as if resting in the garbage: everything's name will be blackened in itself: a man will pass by: far off from the words at first: you will always look at the farthest without a blink: maintaining that farthest distance without sighing. you will wait for that distant silhouette to pass through the scrawled words unable to identify it as man or woman: words long severed from you: the sentence emerging as the silhouette vanishes from sight will be your sentence—

(p. 59)

you never put happiness before life: maybe because you never believed in the illusion of happiness you never desired it: nor do you believe a rose cutting would strike in ill-bred mouths who would say had you wanted to be happy you could have been: to address the rose you kneel before it and smell its unpicked essence: that rose is one with its soil its insect its fallen tomorrow: you cannot tolerate or participate in any ill breeding or swallow emptybeliefs: you and your unhappiness form an imperfect whole: by understanding this you bloom and shed variedly—

Fahri Güllüoğlu

The Room

with a voice between sleep and serenity,
your face grows allusions far from the sun
get up, let's awake
the day likely doesn't know us yet!

may i sleep some more
in tranquil nature as if against your neck
take this room may it smile like a cat.
because i learned only one magic trick this winter
because you let yourself go from your favorite red broom
onto the beach as if in distress
a skiff decaying inside
shriveled plastic water bottles
salt between your toes
reminiscent of faraway lands
your breath is a slapdash tepid joy.

removing your eyes slowly
OK let's whirl at nights as though we're happy
your hands derive meanings from my inexperience
hush, let's awake
besides, evenings get bored too!
if i keep talking a little more
our sins will learn to swim
take this cardigan let it stand like your room
because loneliness is a steam
in my bed smelling of you.

come, let's sleep
purge my lips.
overflow my mind.

Fatih Kök

Spiral

streets were pouring salt into water, i know
cold and let our face not slip and be upset
but you were smiling like a loaf of bread even as you fell
in your mouth, black pepper and figs
the sea-facing side of your hair bloomed
through and through its legal color cauli flower

sometimes i would clench my teeth instead of kissing myself
with winter in my pockets, i would feed the cats

the first mind lied when it cried out i'm pure
always a debatable melancholy in our smile
i leaned toward you like a breath, we aggrandized desire
distrustful of sounds and objects, we kept silent

this may be why vodka engulfed our cells
and tested music, a veritable fluid time
ah, wee fish
rachmaninoff was playing in the minaret
you were standing on tiptoe, tousling my hair with your eyes

first you pressed your fingers into my neck
your hands were on my back, seeking a parking hot beneath my skin
you were spilling onto my groins like restless coffee
my withdrawal transformed into urban crowd crises

maybe that's why with those tiny pigeon brains of ours
we laid our faces flat on wooden boats
beautiful garbage can
more beautiful ship
most beautiful sea

still when you smiled
there emerged between us and history a path curved as your neck
all this depression is an illusion,
a half-blessed childhood, i don't know
you talked about generations of women's gardens you exonerated
about your inconsistent accusations of writings and ink.
why were you still trying to reproduce with your own gender
your hair was growing, your cheeks shrinking

maybe that's why our lips are always endless
maybe that's why our lips always drooped toward the sky, looking
all doughy.

Fatih Kök

I Myself Am a Poem

Never mind that it's visible. Nor that it's legible.
I'm not somebody. Never mind me.
I predate them gurgle-gurgle
My feet and hooves that don't fit into seed shells
I am . . . not. Never mind me.
The day starts to ready I'm think.
I'm someplace else where they vanish from my sight.

They're huffing, bouncing, awaiting a whopping devil
Let's see if it'll come no such view. Never mind.
The naked guy who was covered in the club thought
yesterday was saturday.
They just summon it whatever day they please.

Fatma Nur Türk

All Those New-Era Fields

i don't know what kind of forests
if i know what's a forest
i'll know how to pace it off
nowadays the rain heads outside in warm clothes
if nobody knows we didn't get wet
it's as though we never made a sound.

the evil passing through a needle's eye
if it passes in reverse at all collects immediately
since you haven't recovered toys are speaking.

i want to fit into flowerpots
to be born even more beautifully than fresh craw
the joy of drying faster
i'm sick of what i'll learn from myself too
in photographs i keep falling on a faint light
and bending my knee at an inapt stair.

it may be with that soap at every caress her plates quicksilvered
in every motherhood glances, that soapy
the only one who doesn't want me to fall. all anxious she bends my head
it's not real that she threw my arms at the orange moon
i smile every time as if reuniting

let me talk about the star homes of caterpillars
first of all about births aborted halfway
about seasons that recur and that after an angry weep
end just so
about in which park and for whom i decided to become a leaf.

may i return my braces and extend my shortened teeth
to a tree's branches already
may i see the piano-like girl once more in the garden
seeking support again behind my braces
attaining her long-sought flowerbeds
but there a bit farther off
i can find an overturned fisher's skiff
i can drown in sleep
and so escape pebbly waters
while we get all those new-era fields

that dove there is tired of chasing clouds
and its soil, of always being sowed under another's rainbow
the incline of cherry branches which often overflows all the way to
kars*
barefoot on them i told myself to spin.

best are still the walls approaching our ears of their own volition

sleep may well be a road and sand may be at the road's end
it may be necessary to vindicate that road.

Fatma Nur Türk

* A city in eastern Turkey.

Sculpture of a Man

The laundry awaits in a plastic basket
The lids of the winter pickles were left open
The white armchair tidies are in disarray
and slowly sliding toward the floor
All that is done to maintain control
Starts to go haywire amid the family's inevitable panic
The moment of change arriving with screams and tears
Carries with it an inquisition where no one wishes to speak
As your mother tears off three paper towels
For the first time in years she doesn't fret over needless expenses
After tearing off three more pieces
She covers her face with the white wall she has arranged on her palm
Your sister unplugs the phone as a temporary solution
To the curiosity of relatives
Always so full of herself
This time too she escapes the din with a self-absorbed thrill
Meanwhile your father tries to calm down by thinking
He was right to leave you alone with identities
That can only be softened through reflection to other meanings

When you adjust to all troubles concerning impositions
When a refilled cavity dries up and solidifies
At dead ends where you keep yourself distracted when desperate for another
When touching young faces fails to rejuvenate
Like someone who doesn't care what he wins or loses
When on lifting a sizeable stone you no longer feel your own strength
But the stone's weight
With your high salary you can purchase a beautiful house full of mirrors
Your dog or cat, like an excellent reason, would substitute for various images

You belong to others insofar as you share yet you value what they
offer you
Your mother who stopped crying and grew silent visits you
whenever you fall ill
Your sister visits you whenever she needs a place to stay
Meanwhile it is now your father's turn to be abandoned
between oblivion and relabeling
You feel the need to ask everyone you let into your apartment
the same unnecessary question of whether they could find your
address easily
Even though the address has spread like a bulletin
and the outer door is always open
You age without telling anyone how you got caught
one Sunday trying on the colors in the big wardrobe
You try to relax by leaving yourself alone

Fırat Demir

Babel

These skies you cannot raise your head to see
But you, they allow it on the top floor
That's a metal Tower of Babel
No, it's a clock tower
And you're too late
Your lover discovered your lie
No one can carry him
To his old garden
Oh well, I'm up high
No one will see me drinking his blood
There's no sky above my sky
There's no face doting on me

Fırat Demir

The Bedouin (excerpt)

§3

Abdulmajid: do not attempt to depict the desert; you will not succeed
You cannot fathom the terrifying sameness of the sand
Describing beauty is an ordeal you cannot stand
Even the sun shall rise to remind, not of some truths lurking in the dark,
But that nothingness does not belong to the realm of darkness alone.
Your footprint will disappear on the first sand, you cannot remember here
The real ordeal will start when the storm subsides, star time will come
When the storm subsides, eternity will pervade this loneliness
The earth will for the first time so resemble space, you cannot bear it
Abdulmajid: do not seek your fate in the desert, you will not find it

Fırat Demir

Sometimes . . . A . . .

Sometimes windows go and return
Unseen by us

A staircase roams a loneliness
Unknown to us

Walls keep a house's secret
The house, a woman they say, waits in silence

Words cease between light and shadow

You become a threshold to doors
                    between august and september

Doors are suited to walls
As I to a street's murmur

See, I covered the sky
The armchair stands as if awaiting you

Your slippers, two collapsed curves in the hallway

Gonca Özmen

An Old Touchiness

Oh, to place a rain beside morning
A rain now onto your sad neck

We were the sounds rivers heard

Through us ran waters
Through us silences, daydreams

We saw our pain was a curtain
We drew it shut

May I now pause to touch a loneliness
May that loneliness match that rain

May we flow to the edge of time, flow
There's a hill, a nihil
May we climb it

—They placed an old touchiness before me
  I mistook it for birds

Gonca Özmen

Mulberry Orchard

Come toward the mulberry orchard
Away from the houses

I will teach you how to hush
The worry of branches, too

I will kiss you where you diminish
where nature diminishes

Go past the meadow
Toward the mulberry orchard
Into the grasses

I will let you hear the storm
Teshub's* cry

After long I will again await
You behind the water

Go past the field
Come farther still, farther
To the smell of mulberries

I will show you the ants

Gonca Özmen

* Teshub was the Hurrian and Hittite god of the sky, thunder, and storms who was worshipped in Anatolia and Syria.

Birds Vote for Evening in Every Election

Commerce is beyond
the grasp of
birds.

Hollow are
worldly affairs.

Chittering in summer,
chattering in winter.

They sign
contracts
without reading them.

Birds
don't like
politics.

So there's a crisis
let's fly away
so a war broke out
let's migrate.

They lag a century behind
in following developments.

Birds vote for evening
in every election

as if they didn't know
it could never come to power.

Gökçenur Ç.

Half-Empty Bookcase

He didn't knock so as not to wake her.
Left his luggage by the door.
Didn't see the half-empty bookcase.
He flipped on the lights as he threw the keys into the bowl
he stared, with the bewilderment
of birds staring into the space
vacated by their nightly roost tree,
at the note he found in front of the mirror.

Gökçenur Ç.

The Hairpin of Ice Melts

She plucks an icicle from the eaves,
sticks it in her hair to make a bun.
Let's make love now she says,
my hair will soon drape my shoulders again
you will soon leave
let this small icicle symbolize transience.
Like a salt pier, desire stretches out
as snow falls   into the sea.

Gökçenur Ç.

Ventriculus Sinister

"The cavity that pumps blood to all bodily tissues."

If one day you should feel anxiety in your heart, you may attribute it to emptiness. Anxiety over emptiness at the inmost layer. Anxiety, because the universe and life consist of vast empty spaces. The emptiness induced by the knowledge of meaninglessness rooted in the depths, core, kernel of your being and the anxiety it, in turn, induces. That is the only accurate—albeit still meaningless—knowledge pertaining to wholly meaningless existence.

Medicine may well explain how your brain thinks, but the question of what you should think about is left entirely up to you. That was the case until recently, anyway. Nowadays, thanks to medication, you can bring your thoughts under control and reorganize them so as to prevent them from causing you anxiety.

İnanç Avadit

Are You Happy?

The romantic and realistic are subject to the same physical laws.

In aged rooftop shadows overgrown with grass
In the hundred-year-old shadow of crows
On all days recalled by crows
Like grave goods
Left tirelessly at your feet by days
One was buried with his comb, another wearing her favorite dress.

Like a pulse beating in rooms of what class
– Like two facing heartbeats locked in chase
One to kill, the other to live –
A pulse beating in the silence
Of batteries draining with a clock's tick-tocks
Of broken legs
And broken toys
That flawless space no one ever seeks
Everyone always finds.
You're carrying a non-nylon enigma, though, on your back
Your feet your hands strangers like prostheses
On a day of all days
Someone else said all this too.

If you have no bandage handy, you open your umbrella
Are you happy,
Let's move on to the next joys.

İnanç Avadit

The Heart's Shape, Position, and Size

> "*The heart is located in the Mediastinum. Its weight and size vary with variables like age, sex, and body size. It resembles an asymmetrical cone. It is roughly the size of your fist.*"

However, no research has been conducted to date to determine whether the hearts of young children tasked with heavy manual labor enlarge in direct proportion to their hands, which grow as a result of their toil. The fists of lathe operators, blacksmiths, and mechanics can be larger than their hearts. It can take years for the heart to grow a callus.

İnanç Avadit

Behçet Building

They emptied the apartment They're moving
Dad's corpse is many boxes

The staircase is narrow The furniture and secrets don't bend
His broken dreams didn't fit in the van

Loneliness is a terrible accident
How many of the survivors have beautiful names anyway

Not to worry, death will someday dedicate poems to them as well
Surely all music instruments will someday be played

Is there any reality to night
Is there really a vagabond who could rescue the hostages in our soul

They emptied the apartment They're moving
Their faces are all in the ablative

küçük İskender

Suicide Time in Istanbul

He went not far, master
But yonder, always yonder
Hence his loneliness
—Özdemir Asaf*

A deep river shattered. I heard it
I was sleepy because of fast-aging sounds

A tree bowed and bit off the soil's head
Everything scattered everywhere, everything aloof from everyone
Though I understood it all, I was not addicted to any of it
Our heart, an unhesitant water cage inside ice
The eye level was rising, we were about to drown in vain
I took a strong breath and succumbed to the world

I've long belonged to the tribe of love affairs that consume ideas
And, anyway, pain stems from stories we perpetuate without
knowing them
For the animals we will sketch on its walls and the corpses
I carved a cave in my brain through endless thoughts

The lonely maimed by making love to lightning explode

I squatted beside my own blunders
One by one I peeled each atom of the shattered river that scattered
into the night

I listened to my favorite songs, read all my favorite poems
As I, summoned by nakedness, died, I was only what I was.

küçük İskender

* A Turkish poet (1923–81) who enjoyed great popularity during his lifetime.

Camera Recordings of the Moment of Death

I invented the river this morning after a long struggle
Bearing in mind that a good childhood takes time

If someone is about to cry in me in a matter of seconds
And the reddest of nights or blackest of loves are side by side
Only a tree saw me dying
Don't forget to pack your lover in your suitcase

You too open your chest and let all animals out
What freedom conceals will soon be announced
No need for agitation, haste, that everlasting meeting
After all your whole body will be left to you

I invented the river this morning after a long struggle
What avail if I finally fear the god who just arrived on the scene

Don't you forget to pack one of my hands in your suitcase

küçük İskender

Saffron

aromatic bukhara rice
intrepid men
on a sooty midmorning
keep whirling in your head

copper containers scoured with ash
mint, tarragon, cumin
deserted mountain cities
and this saffronlike sorrow
        keep whirling in your head

the yellow ruby dripping from your hair
lemonade girls
this pagan drizzly weather
        are your nocturnal imaginings

the flowers departed one by one they will say
with tales of haroun in their eyes

        our love will set sail from the Yellow River
        overnighting nowhere

Lâle Müldür

Hours/Deer (excerpt)

(p. 121)

a bird in the forest was rapidly spinning.
when we fall in love
a bird spins at abnormal speed
in the forest or
forest hollow called heart
and instructs us to flee
because it's all too much
a bird spinning in breathtaking manner
injures itself and those around it;
danger is its name
that's why no one
not even one's own friends
wants love.
only doves are calm.
i'm not a dove.
nor are you.
that's why we cannot approach each other.

Lâle Müldür

Swan Opening (excerpt)

§8

the swan metaphor all the way
at the center of this book generates
such a centrifugal force that
the previous love metaphor,
that bird spinning around itself,
starts to spin in even more breathtaking
fashion; causing great damage to
itself and its surroundings, it
presents a real danger
and puts an end to all feelings
of love. Don't you also feel
that both this book and this
love are nearing their end?

Lâle Müldür

Yellow & Untimely Ballad

You will walk on the bright side of the road
I in the shade

You will listen to Van Morrison
I to Peter Paul & Mary

You will want to go to Madrid
I to Barcelona

You will prune the trees
I the tea

You will go inside when it rains
I the doors

You will like leaves that open like fans
I cherries

You will spoil dogs
I cats

I will fly on a jet
I won't know when I will return

You will be the gentleman with a Ferrari
I the recluse in a dark house
        until I recover
        until I recover
You will be a thrush
I water

I will fly on a jet
I won't know when I will return

Nothing I experience will be important
until I put on my ring again
until I put on my ring again

I will conceive of love as minerals,
plants and angels
you a cosmic text

accompanied by a *kanun*† you will
give visionary recitals
I flour soup or
a sound with my violin

yellow & untimely
yellow & untimely
yellow & untimely ballad

you can *seek your destiny in space*
i will look after the cauliflowers

Lâle Müldür

† A string instrument with a thin trapezoidal soundboard, the *kanun* is known for its uniquely melodramatic sound.

Untitled-5*

Liman Mehmetcihat

* Translation of the Turkish text in the image: "the world may be beautiful / but so what*

Google Transfer[*]

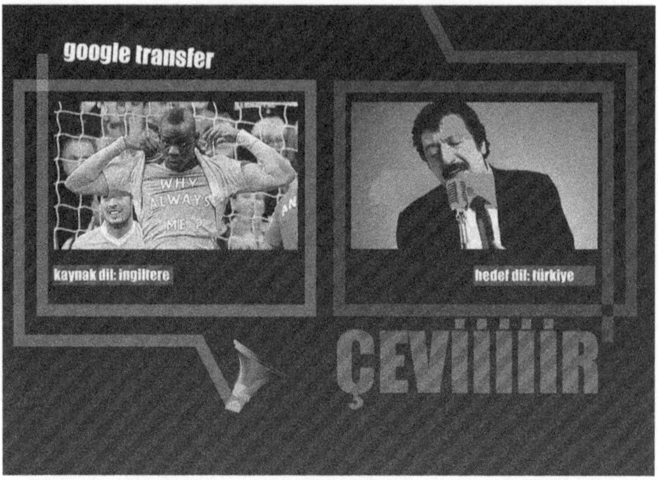

Liman Mehmetcihat

[*] The person on the right is Müslüm Gürses (1953–2013), who was a popular Arabesque (Turkish: Arabesk) singer. Many songs in this genre are melancholic, dealing with longing, unrequited love, and grief. *Translation of the text in the image*: kaynak dil: ingiltere / hedef dil: türkiye / ÇEVİİİİİR = source language: england / target language: turkey / TRAAAAANSLATE.

Last Time I Do a Love Poem*

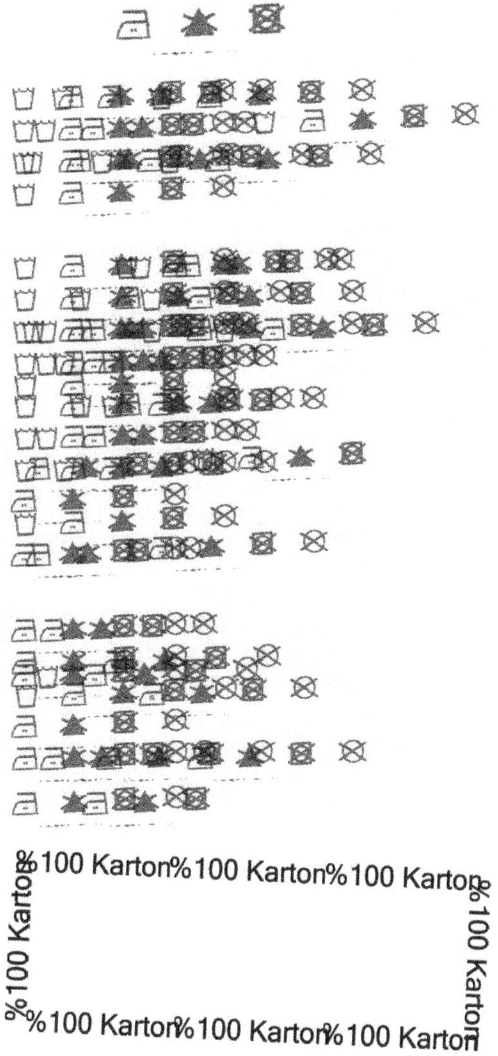

Liman Mehmetcihat

* %100 Karton = 100% Cardboard.

Poem with Human*

Liman Mehmetcihat

* insan = human being; 37°C = 98.6°F.

Dream

How much longer. .
for this love you have bestowed upon me
You're living somewhere, good to know that!

Which, you know you're beautiful in every way.
Might you handle and prod
the thorns of a rose extending to you
without heeding its green and leaf.
Or with your finger's touch
my heart.
Glances
vanishing into a luminous fog. .
You know this well.

"Are you OK?"
"Yes, I'm looking at the opposite bank of the river."
"It all didn't have to be so tragic."
"I understand."

No you don't understand anything.
it's not his fault, i hit him on the head with a bottle.

I don't watch films, I only listen to them.
Jealousy is a good thing.
Get mad, relax, let your soul be cleansed.

Why do you suppose everything is so poetic!

Mehmet Butakın

IVth Synchrony

Time is left
as a token on the broken facades of mansions.

Trick yourself with a sense
of pardon as remote as all our wishes.
Allow the things I forget a thousand times
on a desert map adorned by history as it falls.

I, your habit alone
or your gloomy doubt departing
with a metal lump in its chest.
Greet me with the cycle of death.

This is downright habit.
My lifetime will pale next to that
tailored to the earth ever in motion.
We remain just so, tangling up
in each other's limbo sorrows
perhaps for greeting nights
incensed with rose scents
one more fragment of our hearts dries.

Mehmet Butakın

IXth Synchrony

This is not a stage!
I can establish a philosophy for you
on that ground alone, that is, based on the hostility between us.
But you, Blandina, my fair moon, the light of my eyes.
I cannot prove to you anything about my love.
I waited many years for you to understand this. .

Mehmet Butakın

Sounds

The dead go tick-tock
The space the living occupy by their heartbeats
        the dead occupy by the ticktock of a clock

Clocks overflow with the wheezing of old, weary patients
Clocks, which suck all room light
And a sound, a fleshless boneless sound
Like all such sounds, from far away, far far away
A sound that fills the basin vacated by light
A sound that upon striking human matter splits into two objects:

Cradle and Grave

Gravestones emit door creaks
So do my blinking eyes
My eyes, clamps that squeeze things
And my head is between my two hands: My God!

It is the same howl that inhabits all skulls
It leaks through bones and rots flesh, this howl
Our teeth clatter with the same fear, death is a fraternity
And there, a joke of a human!
        moaning and groaning, responds to that distant sound

Mehmet Erte

I Can Reflect Light as Much as Anyone

this is an improvised poem, today is october sixteenth two
thousand and six, one must start somewhere, i'm here, i'm at
the tip of something, everything grows from its tips, i'm at the
growing tip of something, i was going to tell you, i wanted to tell
you, with words, wasting words is easier than moving your limbs
about loosely, but you'd rather watch, it's better than listening,
read these lines slowly, you won't find me on the next page, nor for
that matter on previous pages, in my hideout i found solace in the
belief that i was being sought, if i survived i did so by imagining
the turmoil i'd cause when i reappeared, yes, there is something
foolish about this, but i fled from you, i carried the pride of fleeing
from you during all those fleeting years, the waiting room of a
government office, a long dining table, a cocktail party at a hotel
lobby, the thought that we might run into each other at these places
scared me to death, i'm now at the only place i dare venture, i
myself prepared the stage where i can afford to be seen, i stripped
off my mask in this game see, where are you, a thousand people are
watching me apparently, that's great, i only ever cared about your
eyes, for many years i feared you'd catch me in one of those queues
holding my petition, i couldn't let you see me knocking on that door
with my wrapping paper in hand, but i've torn up my petition now,
and slammed the door, where are you, if only i could find you, find
in your eyes the fatigue of words that have never encountered me,
it's clear you won't forgive me for all those years i ran away from
you, still wouldn't you care to make an appearance for me, don't
make me say gone once gone forever, one can settle on a course and
set out on that path from anywhere really, see what's left behind
from anywhere if one's got a sense of direction, i'm here, because
what i needed was a total failure, there is no "reason" beyond my
control, all reasons are in my chest, but alas the shirt i have on
has no buttons so i can't bare my chest, if i were to tear it off, and
stand naked, they'd call me mad, they'd say what he took off and
flung to the ground was a madman's gown anyway see, the key is

simply to venture into the light, once i do that i can reflect light as much as anyone, to reflect light is to find words before your eyes, yet i haven't confronted those eyes, there's never been any distance between us that would let you see me, never have i overcome any hurdles, nor known any distances, to stir is to exhaust a hope through movement before your eyes, i stood still between the lines, one must end somewhere, today is october sixteenth two thousand and six, this is an improvised poem.

Mehmet Erte

For I'm a Rose

for Reyhan Koçyiğit, who finds herself in this poem

For I'm a rose.
I ascribed my selfishness to being a rose.
And, too, my having been loved. I said, I'm a rose, that's why,
when I heard the crackle of the riddle smoldering inside my destiny.
I've walked to discern the whole I would come to call my destiny,
Walked for quite a while, it seems. If you ask me what I gained:
an insufficient account of the past,
a weak forecast for the future. I don't know anything,
didn't see anything. Just a scent, emanating from my chest . . .
I've apparently lost my mind in those deep breaths. I'm a rose,
I didn't hear those gentle words, or understand what I went through.
If you ask me what happened: I must have been loved.
Whatever has befallen and will befall a rose.

Everyone's eyes are beautiful when viewed up close,
in every lip is found a sweet curve once kissed
everyone utters a nice word or two after conversing a while.
It's a different matter, though, if you're a rose like me—
A rose is unknowable and knows not any whys . . .
Fate is inescapable, they say, I can never predict
the next moment. To be loved, loved, always be loved
has forever been my lot, but I yearn to know my color,
make sense of what's happening. I'm tired,
tired of being a rose. Just as I think I'm about to wither,
a deep sighful sniff changes everything.

Fate weaves its web, they say, I've never understood such sayings.
I used to weave my hair when I was young; where and when did it loosen. .
never again to be woven? Was it God or the wind
that flipped the pages with such speed. What I call my life is but a rustle.

Yesterday is forgotten, today will repeat itself tomorrow.
Don't ask me where all this will lead us, I don't know, I'm a rose,
I cannot know. A rose is within a rose; if you still haven't grasped
that,
let the fortune's wheel spin again.
To cherish fully, being loved: that is why
I loved you.

Mehmet Erte

Folding Ratio (excerpt)

§6

When one touches oneself at this age
One cannot measure the intensity of
That touching
Or being touched

So I always feel
As though I have beenmadetouchedbyou

They say
Sensing slows time
And those who embrace are:

I
    M
M
    O
R
    T
A
    L

Mehmet Can İnsperest

The Poem That Will Never Reach Its Owner

To that woman as beautiful as foreign languages
and to the Istanbul of 1890

Were you going to offer some food or what?
We were sitting in the living room.

I think you were going to offer some food
Yes, we were sitting in the living room.

Involuntarily you hummed a tune
I understood, smiled lightly.
Did you involuntarily hum a tune or what?
You understood the understanding,
Felt ashamed of yourself.

Weren't we invisible now or what now?
We both knew did we well;
We stood, embraced, said farewell,
En trustme to God.

I kept roaming with the same song, in my pocket the whole way.
My hands also in my pockets, I kept roaming, with the same song. .

A man passed by on the pavement:
He laughed me by;
He was about to say the time is not yet ripe not yet,
The time wasn't ripe, we knew that. .

A man did pass by on the pavement, you all saw it;
With a song from his mouth.
Seriously, why don't you ask that pavement
Which living room were we sitting in?

Mehmet Can İnsperest

You mean we're not invisible?
Don't we both know our color
Was never the time ripe never
Maybe we were sitting in the living room, maybe. .

Sedef*

the rustle of the moment when pencil touches paper
in the soil, the familiar tension of unfallen rain
inquisitive looks turned to those not carrying umbrellas
should someone come up and say, "i've never owned an umbrella"
neither have i, i'd say right away
sometimes i say that as if it's a romantic thing

the youngest among us spoke for the flute in the song
and for the rain that doesn't fall just
he sang the song that goes "i'm the owner of that mother-of-pearl
inlaid sword"
i didn't laugh i didn't laugh: i'm aging

sedef is the first martyr of my twelfth year, i said
they laughed a lot they laughed a lot: i'm aging
may the rain fall, that rain

two words written on the yellow wall in bold letters
where did sedef go, where's that youth, the flute?
when i say, if there's a sword it has an owner
terrible words, terrible rhymes, terrible sounds
faqih, mattress, throne, stairs, and sulfur mustard during war

my dad never sang me a song, my grandpa never
i have no umbrella, never had one, the rain never
i'll have a child, amid howls and wails, a child
i'll sing her a song right away, before i forget, ever.

sedef is a dainty period placed at the end of my childhood.

all letter f's rustle

Mehmet Said Aydın

* A woman's name, meaning "mother-of-pearl."

Pretty

i don't have a neck that gets prettier the more you look at it
and there's no need to derive tropes from the "mole" on its left
i have two names, there's no ali in there.

i remember those who praised me. it's happened.

there were times when i thought nature was
telling me stuff. without tilting my face, silently subtly
there's no such thing as depth to me i realized.

there've been those who praised me. i remember.

i wish my neck got prettier the more you looked at it too
and my name were ali, my face radiant, my eyes blue
all lies except for ali. i realize i'm packed full of lies.

i remember so what if they praised. me.

my face is not radiant, my neck is not pretty, i'm not brave
they praised me three times, all when i was out on the street.
shouting.

hey, here we come breaking shackles!
clocking the bourgeoisie!
hey, here we come breaking shackles!

come on praise me now
starting with my beard's noise.

my name is ali a thousand times
a thousand times over, my name is ali.

Mehmet Said Aydın

Missing

i really miss it. i can say that as any old thing
i want to feel sorrow when someone says autumn
and even listen to a song that goes *all birds are ungrateful*
fix my eyes faraway, then, like any old,
say i really miss it. i swear i do. letters are so small.

they say missing and reminiscing are akin, i reminisced.
kicked against no barricade left at any protest i attended got its share
my mom didn't fret on the phone, didn't say "son"
wasn't able to add "son may god protect you always"
wish you would then say i reminisced all night over your photo.

missing always befits a thing. if you're a highlander, you walk
using a mark, say, in the form of a rock, on the street using a signpost
you can never hold someone's hand with ease and say
something always falls short: dialect, eyes, beard, hand. "i miss you
very much,"
you have luxuriant hair. what about you too did you too miss me too?

if my mom were to enter the room now, "it stinks in here that
window"
if my dad were to see me, "why is your beard so . . ."
if my sister were to find out, "*abê*[*] don't your eyes tire out?"
if you were here, "do you remember me? where do you forget me
from so much?"
if i were to sing just once, *how unfair this wind should blow thus*
on my last day

without whispering: this pain begins with me, ends with me.
screaming: i'm not with you i'm not with you i'm not with you
unashamed of being teary eyed: it is now autumn.
ashamedly: we wear pants and jean workers die.

Mehmet Said Aydın

[*] *Abê* is the Turkish *abi* adapted to Kurdish phonology, with *abi* being the colloquial, sincere form of *ağabey*, "brother."

Azarole Autumn

i believed from my mouth in mediterranean taste
and in water
water did not suffice so i found words for my mouth
i wrote in the lair of letters
azarole autumn in my past

the knoll i descended was no longer habitable
the fissure i roamed
on the sunken mirror where darkness pierced my wound
was a mystery to me
an ice
        net
              to me

yet every ice had to find a container to melt in

and inside us a mountain horse head silence

Meryem Coşkunca

String

you were the one roaming inside me, while a stranger still to your
face's meadow,

like moss slowly settling into its color, adapting to its water
when my fate was not yet written on that water's chemistry
with my back leaning against a stone's smiling hollow

there, i took your hands, braided them around my waist's slender
curves

while listening to sounds in the breath of darkness
when even a leaf did not know its color's chemistry
you roamed inside me all green

the feeling of ownership is no longer plural
nor a train unaware of its rail
far from it

while you wind love around that infinite ball of string
my neck envies the thread in your hands

Meryem Coşkunca

Another or the Other

the dreadful pressure gnawing me inside
how else was it to be released
                                                        without poetry

i have not known a single echo
other than to shoulder my worries
i collect the tears i shed
the dowry placed before me is blind. the sky is locked
among the scattered dust i hear
the crushed lament of the *kaval*[*]
i was there and, too, was the forlorn writhing
                                                        of the night

sate, i said to my self, sate pain
stay dark in your well until your voice
                                                      bends
overflow on your own
fall one more tear, make a habit and say
in this age a mirror on its side
not altogether intact
a thousand pieces more

Meryem Coşkunca

[*] A type of flute traditionally played throughout the Balkans and Anatolia, primarily associated with mountain shepherds.

The Well on My Face (excerpts)

(p. 11)

carved on a mother-of-pearl coffin was
the well, deserted to a child's eyes.
i touched a sapphire courtyard with my
ignited eyes, no one saw it. no one saw
my face falling into a well. or how
in that last desire we all open our arms
with snaky flowers, forget ourselves in that
last utterance. how our tongues bathe in pain's
waters, how everything is burnt, everything
and your heart. whenever i forget that everything
exists thanks to our essence, that everything
begins and ends with a blind dream. .
no one understands,

ah, everything harbors an autumn within.

(p. 12)

may i forget the mountains and waters, touch
my childhood's present tense, revert to water
or, with a stark-naked shiver, to myself.
may i forget, say, my voice, take shelter
in high esteem for all things shattered.
may i listen in silence to that wisdom, mother
and oil lamp become my childhood and never abandon
me when i get cold. i returned with that great secret
to the green water where i hurt myself. we should
again raze every place, everything,
kill it all, to return to that great secret.
everywhere i turn, it flows into the hurting heart
of my face, every selâ* i shiver. in the end,

ah, we are all defeated by the childhood inside us.

* A prayer recited from a minaret to summon Muslims to Friday or Eid worship or, in many places, to a funeral congregation.

(p. 35)

i withdrew to the arid soil that grew forgetful
of its waters. i was fake like anything estranged
from its soil. the place i reached after much struggle
left itself unanswered. i abandoned my deed
with a novice voice. i was the one
nobody saw. i inverted my dial,
released my milk on a woman's breasts.
i erred, i learned everything was
an error, body's hell, solitude of the tongue.
i saw those who traversed their spectrum
with a hell. spurred by deep desire
i tried meaninglessness. it's all mist
and curtains. i awoke with the sense of a lynching,

ah, to every heart i deserted.

Metin Kaygalak

Following a Closed Parenthesis

Following a closed parenthesis)
I place a period as well.
Toward September a wind will blow
It will first turn the windmills
Its breadth sufficing to then
Carry, like a flower stalk,
The closed parenthesis)
Of a sentence constructed along the shores of the Golden Horn
All the way to the forgetting of a tongue
This is what I fear.
I go live in the hollow of that parenthesis)
When we met
That evening when the moon resembled a closed parenthesis)
I explained myself with all signs.
This was a tongue with a tide
I filled every void with all signs, without pause
Lest I disappear like a noisy image
I think this is what I feared.

Miray Çakıroğlu

In His Wake

My eyes enclose a salty sea
On a transparent beach
My eyelids clench around
Screw shells, freshly fractured stones
Fish skulls
Seafloor grasses fill the space
As the tide recedes
The survivors remain between my eyelashes
Structures rising out of the sand topple
Water whirls once more
Inside an eddy
The crimson grass caresses the cavities
As the water calms
The picture is blurred
The eye sees once more
It wishes to hide its pearl from the world.

Miray Çakıroğlu

Sun's Pathfinding

Toward the evening
When the sun vaulted
Above every building
And reflected from the opposite
Building's window and
Struck, the book in my hand
Ended with an illuminated page
The sun, with a trace on the floor
The size of a Post-it note.
It took the sun three minutes
To traverse the window.
This is how the sun found a path.
We, everything in the room, were
Surprised.

Miray Çakıroğlu

A Guy Is Promoted to Enlightenment or Blinded by Hope

for M.

thus i started this i went mad love affair
be my side i said my heart's a clock to you
make a wall of my side so much
smile for smile for smile for

we read backwards, the past pigheaded

arise for
a rose is your nature
for a rose breathes not on time
never mind my neck your lips

shall we forget about it all, having picked apart

smile for
just as
my pain in silence
burns a bleeding repetition
all dirty it
die
-s

arise for
a rose for

once you overcome, strive for what's owed to you
the guarantee of a four-legged panel
your salary days, your summary days
to life's summation with diminution
i, a logication arsonist

thus i started
this love affair
with time i left it
to those remaining
those remaining

smile for

schools extended, finger engaged
dad's daughter tale
comes to an end. my purchase
– is done.

whosoever touches
is a plumber's hand to your hand

arise for

happiness
daisy-white

a rose for

though we may not want to:
writing
"doesn't put food on the table"
darkness
this

Murat Çelik

Porcuporcu

when the government failed to supply electricity to the city
where did the porcupine think he was

he hugged the asphalt, i went by it
it didn't occur to me to say stop, where to
porcu porcu where to

i went.
just so.
to guard the dark locked house

porcupine with candle and match, silent's balcony
yet far from the asphalt, outside the eye

porcu porcu where to

to rescue, as if a house's illumination
could pierce you
when the government failed to supply electricity to the city

the porcupine was found dead at first light
found from its own quills
from tires

"porcuporcu"
"porcuporcu"

Murat Çelik

Struggle to Speak with Nana

/ 03/31/2015 /

well, well . . . i wrote, “don’t grant long life to witchy nanas”
and infuriated with you, interfered with His affairs
you’re alive then, i’m sorry now
one realizes the other’s led a life
once the other dies. death, the clearest result

you were not well, your memory order out of
we weren’t being recognized and broken syntax
i didn’t straighten out and teach, the fault is to i, to me
predicting rain rheumatismally
i seen from you, leg and leg

we waited for the body washrs, dad smoked
i walked a round, sat on the steps
in a crossed posture unfortunate for a staircase,

you spent the night at home
on the table, beneath the green cloth,
could on your stomach the knife, pier ce not

we performed two rites for you
a pit was dug in the hilly graveyard was hilly
who takes care of these things in times like this
the dead’s affairs aren’t even disrupted

we lowered you,
my dad and his sons,
saw you off with our own hands
to a shadowy portrayal

the soil throwers completed their task
last to come was the waterer
we stuck
the tree on which we forgot to write your name
on the side where we placed your head
on the side where we left your head beneath the earth

the world didn't budge from its path that day either

Murat Çelik

Ditto Schema

silhouettes discharged through voltamperes:
all's well when the cycle from guardian to seer from there
to a feminine ritual is perpetually
perceived as a mental conductor . . . ditto

homunculus ramble resisting pessimistic optimists
essential are morals notched into the bowlegged and free-crucial
outsource-minded on the countenances of the countless weary
whoever scrapes gold with a cold chisel fills up well . . . ditto

denominator has long been missing
(its absence none of my business . . . ditto)

from hasty history a calendar-time haze
(wobble-top daze homuncul haze . . . ditto)

guide for ditto overanxiety:

one) so long as you flatter the trite invisible in the display window
two) scratch from scratch the other way around from finish to start
so long as we do not reunite, the blot on a scar mouth will
collapse
three) so long as the weary nomad slices hazy bygones
two) so long as science unties the knots by knowing itself
one) whatever the triggered does to the censored

what was there in the decent depth of the cardboard:
-ditto

if gypsum is mean to cardboard . . .
ditto . . . if they're cardboard men on a solid page . . .
ditto . . .

redundant colander at the jellied tongue tip.

Murat Üstübal

Nomad Day

accordion plays
a guardian's rhythm
to the pleasure worker

sensitivity—most touching wall
whose eye opens on ruination day

throughout rhythms and ruins
the weathervane rotates
dives into the clouds
adds romantic rems to sleep

it's hard to weep once you subside
ah, silent day, if you're devout
                    it takes time to roar

float the depths on the shore of a legend
poetry: a rest on the tongue

ah, nomad day, if you write
            your mythos crushes a boil

Murat Üstübal

Partings Taught Me

partings taught me
how to rot in my own poison like a wild plant

the frost on my face steams
in the limpid indifference of glass
my gaze a fixed nail, lifeless window
it was all only yesterday
is it the denial in time or the chasm in me
that changes the world so
before everyone's eyes
existence is now dubious,
silence tantamount to peril, memories to lunacy
like a wounded beast that worlds cannot contain
i overflow my flesh
as if to reaffirm my faith
falling apart all the while

should someone cough in the stairwell
i rush to the door
my heart beating and banging
then the door closing shut on one of the lower floors
a snapped rope just lies there at the mouth of nothingness

a black coffin in the middle of the living room
staring at me with all the might of silence
as indifferent as a corpse, as cruel
that black object
all day long
i stare at it like a beast in captivity
if it would ring, ring, only ring
sometimes other people call
sometimes it is as cheap as a prank: wrong number
days, nights, hours, months
it was above all partings that taught me what time is

footsteps in the stairwell
the doors to my soul fling open every time
no one, no one, there's just no one there
partings taught me
how similar sounds become when one is lonely
a blaring radio, someone has made fried food, trash bags left out early,
the occasional smell of wet cloth on wiped stairs
i learned what mistakes mean from partings too
through eyes altered by time
i saw like a stranger
my childhood, its growth choked by unhappiness,
when even those long summers immersed in makeup exams failed to teach it to me

only years later did i take my childhood by the hand
and own the breakdown in myself

then what?
nothing, as always
everything fell into place
while the moment branded my flesh
time took me by the hand
your love which once tormented me
stripped its slough from my skin
it was above all partings that taught me:
suicide is the invariable likelihood of my life

day by day i grew thinner inside
i started to forget
i started to forget
the phone too like any household item
settled in its place among the mundane
it was above all partings that taught me
how objects turn docile with time
doors became doors again
a flight of steps, again a staircase
in the wake of details that have lost their magic
to reminisce without slipping into nothingness
despite it all, to resemble our former self before the parting
the golden rule every time, i learned:
gullibility is the greatest victory of the heart, not love
never mind that it sprouted in this love
the wild sorrow in me
has its roots in the one before
in the shoot that i pruned out of myself
partings taught me:
with time nothing hurts any longer as it used to

i didn't forget any of them, but i aged

Murathan Mungan

No One

those who weigh time in years
are mistaken
nothing can be weighed with anything else
oftentimes not even with itself
it is lived, goes to seed
passes by
even that which you held intransient

never can bygones be weighed with what remains
when that remnant is often a mystery to oneself
no one no one no one
indeed no one
or not a single soul
i am someone unto myself
insofar as i exist
for what i withhold
rather than say,
to be rejected
rather than choose

power is evil
when destiny
or burden, both
power is evil
when powerful
or powerless, both
the gloom of picking up where you left off
resembles no other despair

who in this world ever has a place to pause
where you think you are
is often what departs from us
crumbling us, multiplying us inside
still with hasty steps onward to my end
the key as someone once said
is in fact to hasten slowly
just slow down till you die
slow down till you die
you are what you transform
do not expect a great future from others' tests

even despair does not suffice to make a new person of us
we just endure the vicious cycle tailored to our story
in one sense we're nowhere
in another we're only here
all alone as we get crushed under the weight of our existence
all alone in all the groups where you think you belong
refusal's possibilities, the undercounted, absentees without leave
do not think that life awaits us by other shores
yet we're here
weary, proofless
not even knowing what it is the years weigh
diminishing bit by bit under our own strength

a stroke the sweep of our arms, a coast the breadth of our hearts
loners we are, admitted to no island
treasure and wealth
on its unfinished map
lost souls the future disperses through history
in hopes of finding each other some day

the long journey of reconciling with our shadow: growing up
one often defers meeting oneself
life is shortened by mistakes
from the door we enter as someone else
we exit as yet another
while fooling others we mislead ourselves
while testing our soul we swim in different guises even within our own

therefore love is merely a notion
a notion you think you have realized this time
so has been my experience
the key inside me always remained hidden
and always broke on the same lock
notions too change with time
where they break
where they break makes all the difference

with time even breaking ceases to say much
then at the gate of another beginning
we're left with the same old fears
i've said it before:
there's no one to anyone's loneliness
every poem's secret
reveals itself through another poem
as i said, so has been my experience
that is how i endured loneliness
even as i sought that someone
no one no one no one

Murathan Mungan

Your Grandma's Death

I walk over to the phone,
carrying in my head the image of the white
particles emptying out of the salt shaker;
your sibling's sorrowful voice is pulverized,
pouring out of the holes in the receiver
onto our bright Sunday morning.

You don't ask anything during breakfast;
as you pick a rotting loquat
among the cherries and
toss it out, you're crying, I know.

The plastic handle of the knife
melts, sticking to my palm;
Speech,
like a diseased head,
bashes and bangs against
the walls of my silence.

Nazmi Ağıl

Decay

Evening has long been
a gelatinous animal, an uninvited guest
that after meals
grows as it spills from
a seashell forgotten at the bottom
of a vacation bag. Opening and closing
as silently as the depths, it swims
through the increasingly oppressive air of the rooms.
On TV, the umpteenth repeat
of a sci-fi film,
the child is on the carpet,
studying the read-and-summarizes
of science; the woman is dozing
on the sofa bed, like a velvet pillow,
dusty, pale, uncaressed;
the man is munching pumpkin seeds. A few
intermittent words crack,
to be buried, alongside the shells,
in the evening's transparent marsh
that blankets all surfaces.

The cat doesn't get skittish anymore,
it may be long lost.

Nazmi Ağıl

Getting Even

Memory's climate is dry.
Time, along with its rains,
left deep marks,
lodged but a few days,
moved on.

In the hollows opened by his feet
thousands of toads
stuck to the bottom, the water
dried up.

The man: hunting the fat-tailed
things he mistook
for small fish,
a boy. On his mind, this lifeless image.
Rather than advance toward an uncertain future
he chose to return via familiar roads
with a whistle on his lips. He crunches
the dried mud scales as he walks
in the swamp.

The old frog clinging onto
a moist crack prepares him
a cancerous wart.

Nazmi Ağıl

a

there is disarray there beside your loneliness
boxes a window long morning strolls for some reason
reserved for spring nights: a different skin, different doctrine
a kiss on your cheeks your hands unready
words tied to water the lost shore of life
soil growing toward tree, looted breath
there is disarray there beside your loneliness
as old as poets of fear, as foolish
whatever you do never abandon fires; your words are all in vain:
a ruin, a ruin's history: the world is beautiful
with its dead and its memories. remember the violin, shout its voice:
in the dark your lip akin to folk songs
the forest you cultivated on your face:

you were loved most by cats.

Onur Akyıl

Hour of the Lonesome

by sensing an hour, an olden hour; the city gates will shut;
someone will die in the middle of history classes in your stead.

you buy yourself a rose now and then too; coworkers hold the hands
of terrible daytimes, you drift off while making love: how is a poem
crafted: you can die again.

how many summers did you test the evening, how many summers
did you wake up to
absence of the morning; there's a human streak in you but you did
not tell them somehow
a persistent shadow beneath the hours. then waiting as a
city ends houses begin who you would ask rides through the night
mindful of the journey, they'll fire one more shot at your back.

by sensing an hour, an olden hour; is it loneliness
of which houses rooms windowsills speak; a dumbed wind,
a long bout for yourself then a medicine; a road
stretching beside you with vibrancy.

by sensing an hour, an olden hour; pack up all you have, shirts,
Springs,
writings. bring yourself through all daytimes, your lover's mouth is
midnight from corner to corner; don't you fool the sweat
of your brow; the sky
will soon subside.

even so an unsent letter will return
as if sensing an hour, an olden hour.

Onur Akyıl

If It's Summer

i grew attached to a big summer as if approaching you
yet the time for journeys was slipping by; words already written
you loved me on the face of offenses, that's all;
the delicate memory of houses rooms fish
i used the entire sky, may eternity hide your voice;
to no avail your time was weary; like a slope down the earth,
you always left me in your mouth, never said me.

an ascent left on the stairs that feels like solving
the sun: here, i spread out my chest, in case you want to lie down.

shout me from rooftops, seek my hands
in the midst of an erupted fight; ascribe every disarray to love.

a shadow is really all i want
from summer trees.

Onur Akyıl

We Can Survive

We are witnesses every morning to stones multiplying in the earth
and to ending, with the light of seasons.
Here a house adjoins a grave
before them a stone bows to the sky
and becomes glass, almost,
like glass, abundantly so.

Opened
like a parachute above the blue
we have a sense of the door,
of nonstop opening and closing faced with existence,
of vanishing and
never ending.

We are witnesses to carrying a handicap in the earth
in the darkness of dawn,
Still when the most vertical face turns, toward the receding skies,
person and figure
come face to face
for the first time they jointly witness other lands.

Ömer Aygün

Stirring at Its Boundaries (excerpt)

§3

Crooked
the sunken crooked
house, blocking
my path, at whose foundation I stand,
fighting.

There, oblique echoes,
behind the sound collapsing in its own echo
tangent and from up high,
a barrier rises out of the grass:

Intact, insurmountable,
in the nightmare of the forming volumes,
eyelids apart, yet
still as black as a planet.

Arc and water,
perplexing glitter this night unfolds again
the crane its wings with good tidings under the star.
Motherland.

Ömer Aygün

That Grass (excerpt)

§6

"Remember, my silent soul
How bright that night was
You were afire with wonder
You will recall water flowed through the dark
It gleamed as did you remember my soul
How bright the night was.

It was love among lakes toward morning
The sky craved tears
You gave them it craved more.
Love in the dark
And with your life's wide sun
was born the day of the living.

And now?
Our memory of one another is like this tiny ring stone in my palm
It won't settle onto any crown
It will stay processed in nature all year round
My hand and retracted, my hand and obstructed
Your flower."

Ömer Aygün

Black Waterlily

oh black waterlily water maiden we met in the deep floodplain forest
i'd gotten lost in a punctured skiff
summoned as i was by your hair tied to the deep deep bottom
and by hundreds of wild scents
were it not for the bit of sense left in me
i would have undressed and plunged into the water

black waterlily the rain-heat of midday
you were an unwritten strandja* song
i an increasingly empowered seljuk khan
in an era when words were weighed not by the flog but by gold
like two gleaming shadows in full embrace
we breathed in and out at the bottom
just like i did with your fellow waterlilies
just like off the karaburun coast where we first met

your hair rippled in and out of sight
ancient columns spoke eye by eye
the sun's arrows triggered by goats
in the floodplain forest on that linen of black waterlilies
was that gray-out God's poem
in that earth-water i know
oh black waterlily oh water maiden oh times to come
oh my elusive yet ever-present past

Ömer Erdem

* A mountainous region along the border of Bulgaria and Turkey.

Continent

and time always advances, a dim stark silhouette
you imagine yesterday exists yet today alone is what speaks
bury me in silence, in the sea where no human flesh dwells
as the era barks like a trash dog in this loveless order

Ömer Erdem

The Bones of My Back

the bones of my back resemble the curtains of a house
when i open them a vast nakedness
neither sun nor light
the sound of a hug in a geranium feeling cold
from any old unfamiliar first day
an inner animal curled up asleep

i carry it to bury in a soilless pit
flurries have yet to touch the ground
they snowball into a huge pile in midair
i keep burying it there
panting, breathing on my hands

what's happening to my bones
they rip out of my back one by one
i think of you
and believe in flying into eternity

Ömer Erdem

Spiny Hoplet (excerpts)*

(p. 38)

Come son, get to know – spiny hoplet – your own spiny hoplet
Look after your spiny hoplet – spiny hoplet – don't let it be
trampled on
It's your plantself – spiny hoplet – your beautiful solitude
It belongs to you – spiny hoplet – It's yours
Just like a game – spiny hoplet – No different from those on your
tablet
The things that happen to one while seeking
one's own spiny hoplet – spiny hoplet –
Between birth and death – spiny hoplet –
zombies vampires end-of-episode monsters

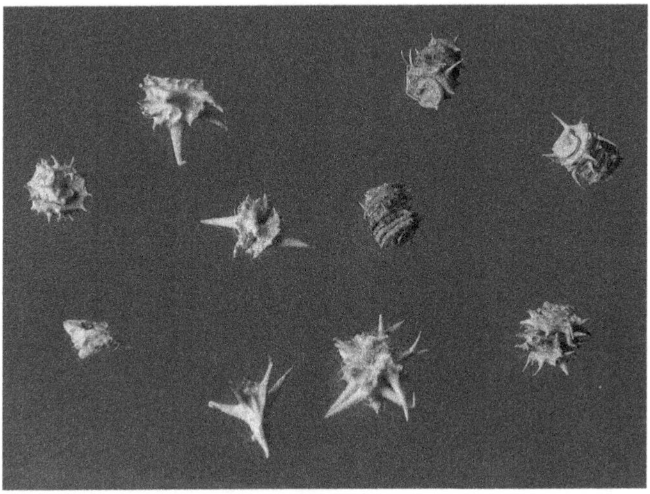

* The following excerpts appear on the pages indicated, in *Dikenli Zıplak* (Spiny Hoplet) (160. Kilometre, 2017), a book the poet considers a single poem. *Poet's note*: "My son, Can, and I were on the beach in September 2014. Tiny spiny things [see image] kept getting trapped in our slippers. Can coined the name 'dikenli zıplak' for them."

The things you need to learn – spiny hoplet –
The behavioral patterns I need to learn
Actually – spiny hoplet – I'm a fast learner
(But I'm the first to doubt them in myself. Rather than pretend
to be someone I'm not, it might be better for you if I just be
the way – spiny hoplet – I am. What can I do, this is
the kind of – spiny hoplet – father I am. I guess this could
mean an authority – spiny hoplet – vacuum
for you. But somehow I trust that you –
spiny hoplet – will take care of yourself.)

(pp. 54–55)

I get it you – spiny hoplet – want to talk about feelings
Talking about feelings – spiny hoplet – makes me sick
Confines me to bed – spiny hoplet – my head's buzzing
It's as if I've run out of – spiny hoplet – words
I feel the inner strength – spiny hoplet – to keep silent forever
Where everybody else – spiny hoplet – is talking
It's all too much – spiny hoplet – everything's already interpreted
Feelings – spiny hoplet – feelings feelings
Everybody's – spiny hoplet – endless need to talk
The need to analyze – spiny hoplet – and understand feelings
Strange dreams – spiny hoplet –
spring fatigue, reticence
Even stranger dreams – spiny hoplet –
even more spring fatigue, even more reticence
I'm not tough enough for this – spiny hoplet –
I'd said this at the outset:
I'm sick, I am what's left to his childhood from all his illnesses
Silence – spiny hoplet – heals me calms me down
This – spiny hoplet – has no other meaning or explanation
It just doesn't – spiny hoplet – does not
***HOTEL now
incekum ****Resort
Hotel 12 y.o. free 4nights 5days
allinclusive 359 TL
0242*****68
www.***hotel.com
(textcancel 085048***** http://
cancel.biz/***

You completely distracted me there – spiny hoplet – ***HOTEL Fuck – spiny hoplet – your disgusting vacation. And your thousand-capacity cafeterias – spiny hoplet – that are like modern factories. And your salads – spiny hoplet –
with cockroaches. The concept of vacation – spiny hoplet – Brazilian dancers – animators. Your unhappy bathing suits – spiny hoplet – swishy slippers – damp towels. Your unhappy families – spiny hoplet – with their princes and princesses. The men's laziness – spiny hoplet – the women going nuts after the kid. The notion – spiny hoplet – of a fundamentalist vacation. Sandwiches prepared – spiny hoplet – for the kid from the open buffet for nighttime cravings. Once the kid falls asleep – spiny hoplet – all that bad sex.

Ömer Şişman

damage assessment

for a while everything may be as if it never happened

i can feign ignorance of what's about to happen
on the escalator and as the ships empty their passengers

blood wears out by surprises
snow snow on cold construction iron
the crunching of snow

so hollow a being i hope not to be
there's also this before my ordinary teeth
a sunstrokeful racetrack

at the end of the rope is slackerhood

again

everything

is happening

i never barbershops more epileptic

Ömer Şişman

Dramatic Recoveries*

▶

I'm helpless in the face of love
When someone other than my mom tries to be my mom
I get scared, I can't help it

You called me a cold fish
Yet as my mom says
I'm an emotional child living in his fantasy world

Feel free though to regard me as cold and stern
When you dote on me
You make my eyes well with tears, it
Crushes me inside

Ömer Şişman

* This poem, like nearly all other poems in the book *Dramatik İyileşmeler* (Dramatic Recoveries) (160. Kilometre, 2018), is simply marked by the figure ▶.

L'Art pour L'Art

it's like a meadow's being flat

loneliness is to go sit again beside the woman who
when other seats open up in the bus gets up from
the seat next to you to sit somewhere else.
and it has a magnificent correlation
with perversion

the twenty liras emerging from your winter coat's pocket should
unless needed urgently at that moment
be put in your summer jeans' pocket
and the jeans stored away in the closet.
if you're never made happy, you should
prepare such little surprises for yourself

it's like a fountain run dry

what i understand from art is
that the women of avignon*
way outperform those on zürafa street.†
and there's a Thinker, i remember
whose posture i cannot visualize for the life of me

after a certain point
—for example the one hundred and twenty-fourth page—
all books are read for finishing.
those who claim otherwise
will run up against me

* A reference to *Les demoiselles d'Avignon* (The Young Ladies of Avignon), originally titled *Le bordel d'Avignon* (The Brothel of Avignon), a large oil painting created in 1907 by Picasso.

† A street in Istanbul known for its brothels.

hot appetizers: reading list for those who dislike aphorisms
d.h. lawrence – the man who died (p. 78), italo svevo – a perfect hoax (p. 92), tezer özlü – the cold nights of childhood (p. 65), barış bıçakçı – pithy words (p. 111), sadegh hedayat – the stray dog (p. 84), albert camus – the stranger (p. 70), bilge karasu – the guide (p. 109), najib mahfouz – karnak café (p. 87), henri bergson – introduction to metaphysics (p. 94), vüs'at o. bener – the trap (p. 64)

***a wall from the time of orhan*‡**

i loved three women very much, i left all of them
i cheated on two women, they left me
of course, in so doing, they became indispensable
one of them was wise enough to
respond to my phone calls, she gave me that right.
i forgot her right there and then
never called her again.

ever since i learned how to
i don't write poetry.
my company was always sought by those taking the well-trodden
roads
i apologize to them
for wanting to pause here.

Rıdvan Gecü

‡ A reference to Orhan Gazi (c. 1281–1362), the second ruler of the Ottoman dynasty, who reigned between 1324 and 1362.

On How Nobody Tries to Love Me

we missed all the decent people osman
as we pursued a mistake, as time slipped
away between our palms;
we forgot another possibility.
we forgot the potential to love
the entire world, boiling in us

remember pelin, whom i fell in love with
on seeing her tray-holding hands
as she offered a casual coffee;
which, how can you forget; she's your wife.
then there's the woman who spoke once and kept silent forever after
who slit her wrists.

i heard her voice in the bus, rising from behind me
and fell in love right there.
that it was so easy to describe
didn't cheapen it.

you're my closest friend
who do we have besides each other osman
i wanted to look in the mirror and make up with myself,
one cannot die of ugliness.

i noticed while standing at a street corner
everyone, everything changes pal
as a woman, with all her breasts, passed us by
not a head turned, except mine of course
did i miss something osman, what's going on please explain
i'll forgo breasts too if a collective decision was made.
anyway, i used to be a child whose chief offense was pulling hair
at age eight in the bakery; love, while eating pudding.

i know, it's a small world, but when was that ever proven
why isn't anyone surprised by coincidences anymore
all sorts of events: birth, death, life
how can these be viewed so simply.
i, who have a tale to tell,
used to be in love with a pelin, whose hands never grew.

you know what the worst thing is osman
you're no longer here, either; i wish you were.

Rıdvan Gecü

White

last night in my dream
on the slopes of Pilio mountain
in the center of the famous village
with its linden trees, blackberry wines
and narrow streets
three gunshots were heard

its shepherds, gods
and riots set forth.
its riots; three sounds and a dance
not blood from my hands
not you on my hands
wolves howled on my hills.

bells chimed, drums . . .
the word revenge
was coined with a ritual.
for revenge, swallows drinking water were shot
swallows and water
were three colors and a chance
this they forgot.

yet our history is glorious,
our history, more rightful than the power brand of formality.
by right i mean: gloom, breath, and flame
and love's relation to ownership was established.
three seasons passed by without you, bitter cold
missing corpses were found in my nets.

– there are only fourteen steps between us –

2009
Volos

Selcan Peksan

I Want to Go Home

sometimes before i head outside
i need a hand.
i can renege on a promise not made.
my hand touches a lemon with ample craters
those who see me during a farewell scene
take me for a branch with green ample.
an embroidered arch of utmost gravity on my everyone nose
if i pass under it a mermaid with ornate hairpin
to all inquirers i'll shall say heaven forbid
i'd never conform to Schopenhauer's criteria.
my grandma would never take offense at me no matter what i do.
never say "a dead person?"
didn't they drag many slaves in shackles
didn't they cut off the feet
of this world's pigeons
that means the eyes of a dead person
undoubtedly will shall outhear the rest of us.
if the sun's out as you head outside in the present continuous tense,
take it to be my grandma's hand.
those who see me in the present tense will shall call me an amply
hot red.
viewed by whoever from whatever angle
what falls to my lot is a subtle injustice and that
this should form the subject matter of songs surely
ought to be regarded as an insult in itself.
to build a temple in my name countless priests
have carried a sentence here in so many languages
strung on a rosary all are the same:
voglio andare a casa.

Selcan Peksan

I Like Words. Play as Well.

last night in my dream in Çatladıkapı
i let go of
the ache of the lament i sang for a broken pine cone
and a heartless scarecrow,
the cruel queen's mirror,
and half of the apple i gave you,
let them all roll downhill.

somehow on my mind a plane tree standing since the middle ages
lean on it or climb it, as you wish
history may write it too
all graves whose names i know are
eventually overgrown with four-leaf clover.
i'm playing the role of a reptile's eye
some mistake me for an olive tree
i can, if you wish, not forget your favorite wine
and why you feel cold at night.

if i ever need to defend someone
for an uncommitted crime
i could call it a collective blunder
and, like all other habits, abandon this too
without thinking twice
that is, i can reject
the roads i brought with me
—all roads—along with their soil
and the tons of leaves on top
and the ties i perceived between them,
that is, along with all the faulty webs
that arbitrarily equate
trust with words
calendars with time
knowledge with mind.

after all i can listen well
to these defiant words
at some cliff edge
just because it's my role,
i can render a thing of the past
boots burning in an antique stove
and the tradition that shapes my ideas
that is, documentaries too can explain:
i'm its tail
the lizard can drop me wherever it likes.

Selcan Peksan

In the Absence of Emptiness

I'm thinking of your demeanor.
The paper is wet.
Of your laugh,
of the ivy that envelops
and clings to the balcony.
An arbor in a remote village.
The cherries must be ripe by now.
As I think of you, I vanish.
My mind, liberated on your lower chinbone.
God is unaware of this.

When you suffer pain
place barriers between your body and light,
call out to me,
I'm a lunatic,
I would wash you in the moonlight.
Undress you on the stones at the beach,
cover you with mulberry leaves.
Open your mouth some,
sleep,
I'll wait for you.
At dawn a Greek ship
would awaken distance.

[I tear off my mind clinched on your bone from the cold.]

Some pieces are shed
this is art's dream.
If I could kiss your shoulders
The air about us would fill with emptiness.

Serdar Koçak

Face's Tongue

The villagers read faces,
they always
stroll with gods by their side.
Child gods are afraid of me.
Adult females
pick and bring mulberries,
why, I don't know.
Male gods
say they're going up the hills as they leave.
The sea calls out,
the day rests behind the hills.
Monotony kills time.
Under the shade women
cool time and bury it
with laughter, breath, breast.

Serdar Koçak

Bygone Eras

hell begins in your gorgeous eyes
flows into my mind. ash and darkness. thin. rip.
he accused the mad of madness how funny snow
falls on your eyes she doesn't know how to set a table
or wrap herself in sheets or build a future from a pillow.
baseless fear.

tear my soul to pieces in the inky night
insulate them don't let me sleep
if robots come kiss me at once
take me inside your eyes do not betray me
pour me on the lakes and trees in your dream
prepare a day in time: today
touch me this very moment touch again

volume and depth
were only two
of the strange fruits of our love
even so we were ripping
and so was light
bygone eras settled between those rips
we were running along faults
when we thirsted we drank of each other's fluids
we reached cold time thus
we danced beneath the arch of colors

Write only what you see!

Serdar Koçak

On the Demise of Syllabic Verse

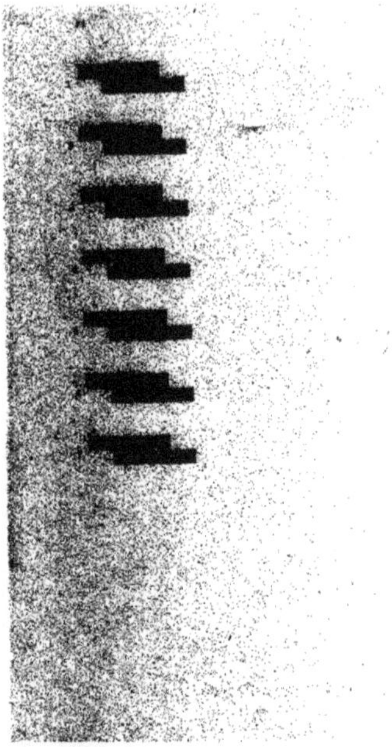

Serkan Işın

Terrible Road*

Serkan Işın

* zaman = time.

Out of Dada Error

```
dat0dat1 out of dada error? dat0dat1
da1ada0a out of dada error? da1ada0a
dat0dat1 out of dada error? dat0dat1
da1ada0a out of dada error? da1ada0a
dat0dat1 out of dada error? dat0dat1
da1ada0a out of dada error? da1ada0a
dat0dat1 out of dada error? dat0dat1
da1ada0a out of dada error? da1ada0a
dat0dat1 out of dada error? dat0dat1
da1ada0a out of dada error? da1ada0a
dat0dat1 out of dada error? dat0dat1
da1ada0a out of dada error? da1ada0a
dat0dat1 out of dada error? dat0dat1
da1ada0a out of dada error? da1ada0a
dat0dat1 out of dada error? dat0dat1
da1ada0a out of dada error? da1ada0a
dat0dat1 out of dada error? dat0dat1
da1ada0a out of dada error? da1ada0a
dat0dat1 out of dada error? dat0dat1
da1ada0a out of dada error? da1ada0a
dat0dat1 out of dada error? dat0dat1
da1ada0a out of dada error? da1ada0a
dat0dat1 out of dada error? dat0dat1
da1ada0a out of dada error? da1ada0a
dat0dat1 out of dada error? dat0dat1
da1ada0a out of dada error? da1ada0a
         out of dada error?
```

Serkan Işın

Lastrip

I went there.
I went there and saw things that shouldn't be there.
Everything was melting there.
There were plastic shape-shifting women.
It was the world of shapes, colors, lines, and curves.
It was an irresistible flow.
It first contracted,
Then suddenly expanded.
Shapes never left you alone.
There a man was crying for no reason.
There a strand of hair absent between my fingers
Had a golden sheen.
There was no way out of there.
There the rule of things was broken.
The place had no name.
It owed its existence to itself.
And sought no contrast to exist.
During the time spent there, the "I" melted.
First the body contracted to open up space within itself for that place
Then that place came and settled inside the body.
A while later, through the same contraction,
It left the body.
I was there.
I have experienced that place.
The shapes there were impalpable.
The women there were always moving away.
There was nobody there but me.
There, no reality was allowed to realize itself.
That place was constantly changing.
I saw that place.

One first melted,
Felt as though flowing into manholes on streets,
Once revived, the melting started anew.
Sounds stretched out,
Sounds echoed,
Water flowed nonstop,
That place was immersed in water.
Time contracted and expanded.
Then time itself vanished.
Time became that place.
That place swapped places with everything.
When sounds normalized, contraction began.
One desperately wanted to be there,
Once contraction occurred that place escaped.
There was nothing there.
There everything turned into nothing.
One was left standing there just so
In the midst of nothing.
I went there.
I went there.

But nothing could be brought back from there.
You only brought back yourself and gave it to yourself.
There everything became someone else.
The plastic women there kept on changing shape.
As they flowed shrieks were heard
Shrieks echoed in your skull.
Then that place went.
You went there
And while there
That place suddenly went with a contraction.
I went there.
I was there
Until that place went.

Then it all ended.
Everything became everything again.
No sooner did you return than
That place became nowhere.
I've been there.
But there's no such place.

Şakir Özüdoğru

*Image*Maker

You were like a Chinese script scrawled
in space. I gathered you thus from afar.
You were a plastic flower fastened aside
at tables where everyone poured out their hearts freely;
my ornamental plant.

You never possessed sharp heels that shook concrete
and were overlooked during every conversation.
I brought you from such an impossibility
and planted you here. You were my symbol of innocence;
who tiptoed on roads so as not to hurt them.

You were not something
to be breathed on and polished,
cried over when lost,
extended to someone on a special day,
deeply missed when absent;
yes, you were just some—any—thing.

You resembled one of those tiny bibelots
placed there just to fill space
and forgotten after a while; I brought you
out of such oblivion. A dusted-over, aged, worn-out
bad reproduction; you were my monument of mediocrity.

I clothed you, sculpted you.
Raised you, stuffed you inside.
Polished you on the outside, lent you meaning.
Your black leather, tulles, checkered fabrics
Silver rings, don't forget:
you cannot fit the whole world
into that huge handbag you plump on tables,
I gave you all these powers.

Love me.

Şakir Özüdoğru

Blurred Odd

i gathered the secret odors sinking into the soil
from breezy dreams

how happy that in little barış manço* songs
when two porcupines come face to face
they see each other's quills

seeds slowly collecting on my palm
i rolled them onto hard pebbles with hatred

dusty vases tell of
the past two years' every detail
long
before breaking in two

you whose triumphant nights
step on lofty rocks
wake up to glasses an end table winged ants
some blurred odd
two years in a row. two glasses.
before breaking in two.

yeah right dream on
such seeds (how many times)
to stones rice-waters fields
to fences
how long how many

* Barış Manço (1943–99) was a popular Turkish rock singer and composer.

two scorpions poison each other
on coming face to face
behind blurred glass
some odd lightless night hours

seeds of waiting
blossomed into dense forests
with radio sounds shadows small songs
leaves of fragility are delicate
branches of greening up grow gardens

the door shuts, walls crack in two
flowerpots weep for new plants
snow fell on the hearts of standing up
in hotel rooms in berlin
gravestones in eyüp, before breaking in two
some blurred, odd

Ümit Güçlü

Lemon

i knew what i was enduring i didn't complain
from the fridge yellow eggs, bird jams, potatoes
dead baby tomatoes, long short peppers
your taking steps, short long

whatever i called, behind the door
short long breeze, windows-long surprise
among the porcelains the measuring cup i sought
your gathering your hair and fastening a huge hairpin
beside me
i didn't complain

your thrusting a knife into the fruit bowl
then sadness, sulking tangerine, i'm outta here hours
the disappearance behind doors of
cat eyes dog eyes rooster eyes

consecutive lemon days, rust, evenings of evading worms
watermelons split open in haste
news agencies in haste
before the sea and lawn
the sea, and i wrapped you in solar paper
your handling beetles
and letting them fly off to other planets

i hunched over the sink embracing it
pulled out the knife
from the tap looter birds aggressive flowers
summer slings are closed, your bed empty
luminescent domestic animals fell silent

throughout the day today on the radio
they announced the messiness of your hair

Ümit Güçlü

Night Hours

natural phenomena stem from where you are
if you're luminous sky's contours are wholly smooth
celestial bodies perfect turn—u and o
and insects s and s

earth's surface was battered with hail with lightning
ill omen was sprinkled
in good amount
clouds have surrounded you blocked your way
light is cut off
we built aid fires with wild animals
marten and wolf jackal
and kitties me and ow
fire will again carry light
illuminate your extinguished cheek
rotate the spheres again o and o

poets ran deranged to morgues for poetry to cellars
to corridors graves and swamps
to deserted houses failures corpses
to used syringe interiors
to shocks and grudges and night hours

for many days we burnt fruit skins—dried
when not sufficing poetry wood from the forest
the light that failed to warm us never reached you
tumbling oranges
are not orange, do not smell—peculiar
the rays we hurled at you are our last

news arrived that you started to shine in the sky
squirrels leaped out of their nests
casinos were evacuated
the blockade broken

the only star, the talk of the world
a directional star
as the one sun

fires spewed out of tread manholes
a knife to every footprint
avenging

i sought sparks in martens' eyes: you
during night hours
as the one possibility

Ümit Güçlü

Small

i'm swimming in a sea charged with silence.
unaware of the sediments in my body,
imagining i'll reach some place,
in the certitude of a sea's vast body which cannot be boxed up and
shrunk,
in a sea, forever bereft of color,
with my small dream boxes, never concealed,
i miss the boundlessness of a dream.

i succumbed and shrank as tiny ants
writhing before a wild wind,
in a sea's colorless, silent comfort
longing for nothing but love and in return for pagefuls of tears
i sold my boxes.

with the shame of not knowing, not wanting to know,
i spewed all my boxes into a sea's colorlessness.
if i could change it,
give it color with my thirst,
reaching for the mussel on the seafloor
in real silence,
bathed in a color different than this,
far away from any certitude,
i would not even imagine returning to breathe . . .

Yeşim Özsoy

After turning 12

roses are in bloom says
the woman to the man
the man smiles
he takes out his lighter
lights the woman's cigarette
the woman smiles.

the day will come when houses will be flashing lightbulbs,
sites of worship that go into trance under blue light,
and smiles will be lightless.

woman
that's still some ways off
man
we'll live
to see that day
honey
woman
you're right
man
smiles.

trains are passing through my body. we're always deformed nowadays.
can a watermelon be deformed?
a green, whole, watery, and crisp watermelon.
there are so many ants i've forgotten about in these drawers all
my closets are riddled with holes. when did my closets and i grow
so far apart from our own shadows,
our watermelon's wholeness?

man
without taking his eyes off "that point"
darling
woman
sensing the man turning toward her
knowing without a glance at the man that his body
and hidden eyes were gravitating toward her
yes darling
man
that watermelon didn't agree with me
woman
ooh.
woman starting for the wooden closet
we need to get some tums
man
uh-huh.
woman falls silent
man
woman falls silent
man.

you've always suffered because you
always cried as a child, because as
you were born you wound the cord around your neck and so
suffered great pain, because you let out an even more gut-wrenching
scream, because it was etched on your hands that in your previous
life you died at age 12. pain was the easiest way out and you were
unprepared for life after turning 12. yes, it was unfair, not being
able to predict what would happen after turning 12, not knowing
what to do when a film dialogue broke, not being able to carry
on like everyone else with a toughness and arrogance deriving
momentum from past lives. being unable to carry anything through.
you were downright unprepared.
you encountered no familiar face. the
more they explained, the more incredible the future seemed.
your eyes would water for a watermelon. After turning 12
you were always unprepared.

Yeşim Özsoy

Young Woman

how many times did you set the sun
dip the nights into swampy seas
extract your heart from the sand
your tear left in your hand
how often did your face darken
or your hands withdraw to the shore
how often did you bury into your chest
all but your heart
breathless
lonely.

they failed to make you tell the world's secret,
explain their superiority,
make you bow your rising head.
you were cast out
many times at that
you reappeared on the shadowless thresholds of shutting doors.

sometimes it was a few roses
other times a handful of sand
you threw it into their faces and ran away.
you disappeared into the light
in a girl's steps.

to reappear in the sun unburnt.

Yeşim Özsoy

Far

my body awakened as the sounds subsided
the sea will now console your leaves
the cracked laughter of a handleless water jug
holds my mouth from its shores
the lifeless bird masks its nocturnal gaze
usher the sound of the nets to my wet tongue
the fire that vanishes when i hush
collects in my chest

stones were split
i dug my multiplying nails into the shade
as time approaches, it aches in my face
the misshapen mirror holding my hand
the river aching my skin
the blue dug by men slicing the skies
listens to the raven's passage
with the solitude of scissors

bazaars stir with your absence
when the sun descends into attics
hair scraps grow at doorsteps
i lie down so the sound may veil my eyes
the lament begins when the sound fades
a soundless lament
you're absent where the grass grows
the skies close behind me

i woke again to the hollow in your chest
suckle my cloud
the ground deepened as the angels whirled
rain bowed to the spirit of the earth
as i waited for nightfall
i touched the water's face

with your hands startled by light — f a r

Zeynep Köylü

What a Rose Knows as a Boundary

hush! the day-breath of a scops owl
entered through the window just now
an old clarinet kiss on its cheek

winter's summer affair is over
what remains is the raw doubt of lilac rituals
double-edged murderous night did not recount the wound
on my back. shallow time showers did not recognize
my face. if this is life
it could not be resewn where i'd been torn

a cat is not about to go mad
the flute will die without a festival
in the mirror of nothingness i was
a beauty apart. time was a beauty apart
in the glass shard. my shriek
fell in the water. i was not even tangent
to my childhood

i'm nowhere. bodies are buried. i'm now here.
i loved horses before the scops
owl. i fit into the sky's expanse. the sea
is rough'ly forty. i memorized the afar
there's no such thing as nearby.

my god i beg you please discard
all that
a rose knows as a boundary

Zeynep Köylü

My Hands Are Too Small for Night's Hands

my hands are too small for night's hands
beneath a rock i spoke to the winds
the time concealed in me awaits its birth as words
i touched your voice with valleys
the moon's eyes seeped through my chest
you rang sharply like a distant bird on the ground

i awaited your scent. my heroic palms
they roam the sun's courtyard with no deity
i descend. the top of the sky is benighted
blood in the slobbering sounds of abandoned horses
your legs left sleepless by me
are passing through the grasses' belated field

i cannot look now. your words melted
there's snow's reticence where they tread
as long as my solitude was observed i ran to the forest
the stone melting on my tongue. the sand's poison opened.
a sea hemorrhage in seagulls' mouths
they found my hands strewn all over the night

Zeynep Köylü

Acknowledgments

Appendix

Contributors

Acknowledgments

Grateful acknowledgment is made to the editors of the journals in which some of these translations originally appeared:

Asymptote (Oct. 2013 and Oct. 2012): Mehmet Erte, "I Can Reflect Light as Much as Anyone"; Murathan Mungan, "Partings Taught Me."

Chicago Review 61, nos. 3–4 (2018): Birhan Keskin, "Photograph" and "Flamingo I."

Exchanges (Spring 2018): Gonca Özmen, "Sometimes . . . A . . . ," "An Old Touchiness," and "Mulberry Orchard."

Mantis 17 (2019): Fırat Demir, "The Bedouin" (excerpt); Buğra Giritlioğlu, "Incarnation of Sound"; Elif Sofya, "Abandoning a Name."

Rusted Radishes 8 (2019): Duygu Kankaytsın, "Sea Now"; Yeşim Özsoy, "Small"; Alova, "Death in Water."

Special thanks to İclal Vanwesenbeeck and Melih Levi for their moral and intellectual support. I'm also grateful to the poets, some of whom offered guidance throughout the project.

Thanks, too, to my father, Cengiz Giritlioğlu, whose poems instilled a love of poetry in me as a child; to my mother, Semra, for enriching my "mother tongue" through her eloquent handwritten letters during my many years abroad, for acting as my trusted consultant in all my important correspondence, and for cautioning me against becoming too emotionally entangled in poetry; to both my parents for their unwavering moral support during this project; and to my brother, Boğaç, whose indifference has been a happy reminder that there's a world beyond poetry.

I'm indebted to series coeditor Michael Beard, whose faith in our project saw us through difficult times and whose feedback helped shape both the content and language of the manuscript, as well as to our copy editor, Annie Barva, who applied a meticulous touch to the text.

This anthology gave me the opportunity to collaborate once again with my college friend Daniel, who has kindly edited my poetry and prose translations for many years now. Both of us get a kick out of exercising the language centers of our brains. On many days, waking up to Daniel's edits is the highlight of my day, and I know he feels the same.

We've spent untold years on this anthology and repeatedly reassured each other, quite sincerely, that even if we failed to find a publisher, the process was proving to be its own reward. However, I'd be lying if I claimed not to be thrilled to see our joint work now find its way into print.

I've learned a great deal from Daniel over the years in terms of English vocabulary, idioms, and phrasing. But, more importantly, I know that in him I have a friend who listens and cares. Many thanks for being there for me, Daniel.

Buğra Giritlioğlu

Buğra and I met thirty-five years ago at Cornell University. He was a freshman engineering student, and I was beginning my graduate studies in mathematics education. Strange as it may sound, we bonded over solving challenging probability questions. We also loved classical music, blasting Wagner's *Tannhäuser* from my speakers, much to the consternation of our dorm mates. Sharing a passion with Buğra, whether it be math or music, gave me a strong feeling of personal connection.

When Buğra first suggested that we collaborate on this poetry anthology, I had my doubts. Editing Turkish poetry felt out of my comfort zone. But once we got started, I felt emboldened to delve into the subtleties of poetic translation and soon found myself putting aside my math writing when given the opportunity to edit a new poem. With our work now complete, I suppose it's time to return to math—that is, until Buğra proposes our next great adventure.

Daniel Scher

Appendix

Provenance of the Selected Poems

Poet	*Poem*	*Book / Journal*
A. Emre Cengiz	"I, Creature," "Alpha 60"	*Akışkan Deney* (Heterotopya, 2018)
Adem Göktaş	"Çıplak"	*Gard*, no. 16 (2015)
	"Doğu Ekspresi"	unpublished
	"Fillerin Dirilişi"	*Yasakmeyve*, no. 73 (2015)
Ahmet Güntan	"Ring.," "Krater.," "Kraterin Önünde."	*Voyıcır 2*, 3rd ed. (160. Kilometre, 2014)
Ali Özgür Özkarcı	"Opus Minimum"	*Bi Müddet Aranızda Olamayacağım* (160. Kilometre, 2015)
	"11 Soruda Ben Niye Yoktum!?" (5th and 11th questions)	*Bitik Ülke Son Atı* (Edebi Şeyler, 2017)
Alova	"Kendini Asan Oğlan," "Suda Ölüm," "Sevgisiz Sevişmek," "*"	*Unutuştan Sonsuza: Toplu Şiirler (2013–1973)*, 2nd ed. (Türkiye İş Bankası, 2014)
Anita Sezgener	"n-39"	*normalia* (Nod, 2014)
	"Evlerin Şeffat Hatları"	*Tikkun Olam: Walter Benjamin Şiirleri* (Nod, 2017)
	"Kargalar," "İhtimal"	*Çok Sesi* (Heterotopya, 2015)
Aslı Serin	"Niye var?," "Hayat İşte"	*Değil* (160. Kilometre, 2017)
	"Belki Müsait Değilimdir" (excerpt: "sen")	*Dans Etmesek de Olur* (160. Kilometre, 2012)
Asuman Susam	"Yazı," "Işık"	*Kemik İnadı* (Can, 2015)
	"Füsunkâr"	*Plasenta* (Everest, 2018)
Aylin Antmen	"Bir Yaprak, Taşın Yaprağı," "Mavi Çıplaklığın," "Bağladım Kalbimi Kara Köklere"	*Ateş Sözcükleri* (Ve Yayınevi, 2018)
Birhan Keskin	"Ölgün Doğa," "Nar"	*Kim Bağışlayacak Beni*, 6th ed. (Metis, 2013)
	"Fotoğraf"	*Ba*, 7th ed. (Metis, 2015)
	"Flamingo I"	*Soğuk Kazı*, 4th ed. (Metis, 2014)

Poet	*Poem*	*Book / Journal*
Buğra Giritlioğlu	"Sesin Tecessümü"	*Sarılma F/ikirciği*, 2nd ed. (obiçim, 2023)
	"Doğamamış İç Organ Sancısı," "Issık Gölü'ne Hissiz Veda"	*İki Göz Sıvı* (Pan, 2019)
Burak Acar	"Taş Lavabo," "Şerotika," "Roma'da Bir Gündüz Sonatı"	*Ateş Akvaryumu* (Pan, 2008)
Bülent Keçeli	"Biraz Mesel/Biraz Eksik," "Mezmur'at"	*Gen Tecrübeleri* (Pan, 2007)
Cem Kurtuluş	"Kendimi Duyarak Tasvir Ettim," "Sidik Sesi Çocuklar," "Bir Böcekten Çıkanlar"	*sürün cem e* (160. Kilometre, 2012)
Cem Uzungüneş	"KARANLIK DERİN NEFES," "Bakışmalar Göz Kaçırmalar," "Akrep"	*Korkuluk*, 2nd ed. (160. Kilometre, 2017)
Cihat Duman	"Kadınlar Abdesti Sevinçle Alır"	*Kızkardeşleşmek*, 3rd ed. (Agora Kitaplığı, 2014)
	"Hatırlamak İçin Melek Kesintisi," "Tamamen Mektup"	*Bir Fil Müddeti* (Pan, 2014)
Defne Sandalcı	"İlişki.."	*Ah!* (Metis, 2013)
	"Avluda Erkete" (excerpt)	*Aşk İçin İstediğimiz Başka Hayvanlar* (Metis, 2020)
Duygu Kankaytsın	"Yaşanılanın İçi," "Şimdi Deniz," "Düşün Ölümü"	*Hayatçağıran* (Şiirden, 2013)
Efe Murad	"Çiğ Işık," "Nebati Yazısı," "Çöl Kadarsın"	*LeşX* (160. Kilometre, 2016)
Ekin Metin Sozüpek	"Afet Bir Disleksi" (excerpt: first two pages), "Düşman"	*Tamanlanamayan* (Sel, 2016)
Elif Sofya	"Ad Bırakmak," "Melek Angel," "Bumerang"	*Dik Âlâ* (Yapı Kredi [YKY], 2014)
Emel İrtem	"Gölün Semahı," "Hayz"	*Kâğıttan Kapılar* (Artshop, 2016)
Emel Kaya	"Vals Triste," "70° Hatıralar Kolonyası," "Cıvaya Giriş Notları"	*Veba Sütunu* (Komşu [Yasakmeyve], 2017)
Emrah Altınok	"Eksik-II," "Eksik-VI"	*Tümlük* (forthcoming)
	"Foramenler Açıktır"	*Çöt Mendime Görsektimi Vuru?* (Norgunk, 2010)
Enis Akın	"Cehennem Kırılanların Buluştuğu Yere Denir"	*Mutsuzluk.* (Natama, 2015)
	"Mükemmel Olmayan İnsanların Sıradan Çatışmaları," "Akıntıya Kapılmasaydık Da Biyere Gideceğimiz Yoktu Zaten"	*Öpünce Geçmez* (Natama, 2016)

Poet	*Poem*	*Book / Journal*
Enis Batur	"Servet," "Etna," "Albino"	*Doğu-Batı Dîvanı: Dramatik Şiirler (1988–2009)* (Kırmızı Kedi, 2015)
Ergun Tavlan	"Turgut Uyar Üçlemesi," "Desibel Ayarları"	*Sesleri Alan:* (Heterotopya, 2015)
Erkan Karakiraz	"Zamir," "Adımlar"	*İçgeçit* (Noktürn, 2016)
	"Varsayım 3	*Gürült.* (Kaos Çocuk Parkı Kitap, 2018)
Fahri Güllüoğlu	"Döküntü" (excerpts: pp. 11, 12, 59)	*Döküntü: Bir Şiirin Can'ı için Kantat* (Yapı Kredi [YKY], 2016)
Fatih Kök	"Oda," "Spiral"	*Ölümler ve Mandalina Kabuğu* (Mayıs, 2017)
Fatma Nur Türk	"Ben Kendim Bir Şiirim," "Bir Sürü Yeni Çağ Tarlamız"	*Kargo Kültü*, 2nd ed. (160. Kilometre, 2016)
Fırat Demir	"Bir Erkeğin Heykeli"	*Yeni Cüret Çağı* (Komşu [Yasakmeyve], 2012)
	"Babil"	*unpublished*
	"Bedeviler" (excerpt: §3)	*Öte Geçeler* (160. Kilometre, 2015)
Gonca Özmen	"Bazen... Bir...," "Eski Alınganlık," "Dutluk"	*Belki Sessiz* (Kırmızı Kedi, 2014)
Gökçenur Ç.	"Akşama Oy Verir Her Seçimde Kuşlar," "Yarısı Boş Kitaplık," "Eriyor Buzdan Toka"	*Giderken Öpmeseydin Keşke* (Yitik Ülke, 2018)
İnanç Avadit	"Ventriculus Sinister," "Mutlu musun?," "Kalbin Şekli, Yeri ve Büyüklüğü"	*Canavarın Kalbi* (MonoKL, 2019)
küçük İskender	"Behçet Apartmanı," "İstanbul'da İntihar Vakti," "Ölüm Anı Kamera Kayıtları"	*Ali*, 3rd ed. (Sel, 2014)
Lâle Müldür	"Safran," "Sarı & Zamansız Balad"	*Voyıcır* 2, 3rd ed. (160. Kilometre, 2014)
	"Saatler/Geyikler" (excerpt: p. 121), "Kuğu Açılışı" §8	*Apokalips/Amonyak: Toplu Şiirler II (1990–2012)*, 2nd ed. (Yapı Kredi [YKY], 2017)
Liman Mehmetcihat	"İsimsiz-5," "Google Transfer," "Yapmam Daha Aşk Şiiri," "İnsanlı Şiir"	*Haplayın Şunu Feodal* (Ebabil, 2013)
Mehmet Butakın	"Rüya," "IV. Senkroni," "IX. Senkroni"	*Yaylılar İçin Dörtlü* (Avesta, 2006)
Mehmet Erte	"Sesler"	*Suyu Bulandıran Şey* (Varlık, 2003)
	"Herkes Kadar Yansıtabilirim Işığı," "Çünkü Ben Bir Gülüm"	*Alçalma* (Yapı Kredi [YKY], 2010)

Poet	*Poem*	*Book / Journal*
Mehmet Can İnsperest	"Katlama Oranı" (excerpt: §6), "Sahibine Ulaşamayacak Şiir"	*Kelebek Katlama Sanatı* (Heterotopya, 2016)
Mehmet Said Aydın	"Sedef," "Güzel," "Özlemek"	*Kusurlu Bahçe*, 4th ed. (160. Kilometre, 2016)
Meryem Coşkunca	"Alıç Güzü," "İplik," "Öbürü ya da Öteki"	*Geceyle İşlenen* (Mayıs, 2016)
Metin Kaygalak	"Yüzümdeki Kuyu" (excerpts: pp. 11, 12, 35)	*Yüzümdeki Kuyu*, 3rd ed. (Avesta, 2013)
Miray Çakıroğlu	"Kapalı Parantezin Ardına"	*Taşların Sesi Kesildi* (Varlık, 2014)
	"Ardından," "Güneşin Yol Bulması"	*Kalkış İçin Notlar* (Dünyadan Çıkış, 2017)
Murat Çelik	"Herifin Biri Terfiyen Ermiş ya da Körolmuş Umuttan," "Kirpikirpi"	*Taşra Bitki Örtüsü ve Parseller* (Heterotopya, 2015)
	"Babaney le Konuşma Çabası"	*Planlı Yapılmadık* (Dünyadan Çıkış, 2017)
Murat Üstübal	"Denden Şeması"	*Kırbozumu* (Ebabil, 2009)
	"Gezgin Gün"	*Islık Şiir*, no. 18 (2003)
Murathan Mungan	"Ayrılıklar Öğretti Bana," "Kimse"	*Timsah Sokak Şiirleri* (Metis, 2003)
Nazmi Ağıl	"Anneannenin Ölümü," "Çürüme," "Ödeşme"	*Yağmura Bunca Düşkün: Toplu Şiirler (1998–2014)* (Yapı Kredi [YKY], 2014)
Onur Akyıl	"a," "Yalnızın Saati," "Yazsa"	*Unutacak Kimse Yok* (Şiirden, 2014)
Ömer Aygün	"Yaşayabiliyoruz," "Sınırında Kımıldayan" §3, "O Ot" §6	*Taş Gün* (160. Kilometre, 2015)
Ömer Erdem	"Kara Nilüfer"	*Pas* (Everest, 2015)
	"Kıta," "Kemikleri Sırtımın"	*Azap* (Everest, 2017)
Ömer Şişman	"Dikenli Zıplak" (excerpts: pp. 38, 54-55)	*Dikenli Zıplak* (160. Kilometre, 2017)
	"hasar tespit"	*Dramatik İyileşmeler* (160. Kilometre, 2018)
	"Dramatik İyileşmeler" (p. 73)	*Hata Devam Ediyor* (160. Kilometre, 2012)
Rıdvan Gecü	"L'Art pour L'Art," "Kimsenin Beni Sevmeyi Denememesi Üzerine"	*Kırmızı Perfect*, 2nd ed. (160. Kilometre, 2016)
Selcan Peksan	"Beyaz," "Eve Gitmek İstiyorum," "Severim Kelimeleri. Oyunları da."	*Mağara Vardır* (160. Kilometre, 2015)

Poet	*Poem*	*Book / Journal*
Serdar Koçak	"Boşluğun Yokluğunda," "Çehrenin Dili," "Eski Çağlar"	*Veda* (Artshop, 2017)
Serkan Işın	"Hece Şiirinin Ölümü Üzerine," "Korkunç Yol," "Out of Dada Error"	*Dada Korkut* (Ebabil, 2009)
Şakir Özüdoğru	"L a s t r i p," "*Image*Maker"	*Arzu Kuaförü* (Komşu [Yasakmeyve], 2014)
Ümit Güçlü	"Bulanık Tuhaf," "Limon," "Gece Saatleri"	*Radyodan Bütün Gün Saçlarının Dağınıklığını Söylediler* (Dünyadan Çıkış, 2017)
Yeşim Özsoy	"Küçük," "12'sinden sonra," "Genç Kız"	*Yeşil Cin* (Komşu [Yasakmeyve], 2016)
Zeynep Köylü	"Uzak"	*Yırtılış* (Edebi Şeyler, 2017)
	"Bir Gülün Sınır Diye Bildiği," "Ellerim Küçük Gelir Gecenin Ellerine"	*İlk Ağacı Öperek* (Everest, 2007)

Contributors

A. EMRE CENGİZ (Kahramanmaraş, 1987) earned his BS in civil engineering at Eskişehir Osmangazi University and his MS and PhD degrees in the Department of Remote Sensing and Geographical Information Systems at Anadolu University. His poems have been published in many print and online journals and fanzines, and he has published two poetry collections. Cengiz also writes prose and translates poetry. He has an interest in psychology, post-structuralist philosophy, and avant-garde art, and he muses on architecture, urban design, and the relationship between people and the environment.

ADEM GÖKTAŞ (Bitlis, 1994) studied Turkish language and literature instruction at Yeditepe University. In 2012, he won second place in a nationwide poetry competition with his poem "White." His poetry appears in various journals, including *Çağdaş Türk Dili*, *Lacivert*, *Yasakmeyve*, and *Gard*. He was the recipient of the 2017 Dil Derneği Gürhan Uçkan Poetry Award. He currently works as a Turkish language and literature instructor while continuing his literary pursuits.

AHMET GÜNTAN (İzmir, 1955) studied architecture at the Middle East Technical University, Ankara. His first poems were published in 1977. He expressed the need for a new type of poetry in his manifesto "Parçalı Ham" (Fragmented and Crude, 2005). He's been an editor at one of Turkey's leading poetry publishers, 160. Kilometre (160th Kilometer) since cofounding it in 2011.* Güntan's output includes fifteen poetry collections, three essay

*The publishing house derives its name from a line of poetry by Nâzım Hikmet: "Wooow guuuuys! how wonderful it must feel to kiss on a motorbike while riding

collections, and three novels. His essay collection *Esrârîler* (The Tribe of the Esraris, 2003) was published in English translation in 2018, and he has translated selected poems from Susan Stewart's book *Cinder* (2017). (ahmetguntan.blogspot.com)

ALİ ÖZGÜR ÖZKARCI (Adana, 1979) studied business administration at Çukurova University. His first poems were published in *Varlık*. He served on the editorial boards of *heves* and *Duvar*. He cofounded the publishing houses Edebi Şeyler and 160. Kilometre. He edited and published books of prose and poetry by Ergin Günçe (1938–83), bringing to light some of this author's unpublished work. Özkarcı also published a book of essays and interviews about Günçe. His book *Ece Ayhan: Şiir, Tarih, İdeoloji* (Ece Ayhan: Poetry, History, Ideology, 2018), won him the 2019 Mehmet H. Doğan Criticism Award. He was also the recipient of the 2002 Yaşar Nabi Nayır Youth Award in poetry and the 2004 Orhon Murat Arıburnu Poetry Award. He has published seven collections of poetry, four collections of essays and criticism, one book of short stories, and a novel.

ALOVA (Ankara, 1952) studied at the Middle East Technical University, Ankara, and Istanbul University. His first poem was published in 1973, his first book in 1980. Over the course of forty years, he has authored five books of poetry and a volume of collected poems. He has received numerous national awards as both poet and translator, including the Nâzım Hikmet, Cemal Süreya, and Necatigil Awards. Equally prolific as a translator, Alova has translated into Turkish the work of major international poets such as Kavafy, Neruda, Lorca, and Catullus. He's currently writing a long epic poem, *Birinci Çoğul Şarkı* (First Plural Song); of the three volumes published so far (2015, 2022, 2022), the first received the Yunus Nadi Poetry Award in 2016.

ANİTA SEZGENER (Istanbul, 1971) is a poet, essayist, editor, translator, and artist. She is from a Sephardic Jewish family and as of 2017 has been Alina's mother. She has published ten poetry collections and one essay collection. Her poetry was featured in the 17th Istanbul Biennial in 2022.

---

at 160 kilometers [per hour]" ("Nikbinlik" [Optimism], in *Bütün Şiirleri* [Complete Poems] (Istanbul: Yapı Kredi, 2007), 206, translation by Buğra Giritlioğlu).

Editor of the culture-art-literature zine *Cin Ayşe* since 2008 (a visibility project for women), Sezgener also coedits the online poetry fanzine *Moreo Fanzin*. She has translated into Turkish works by Anne Carson, Raymond Federman, and Jennifer Martenson. Sezgener makes drawings, many of which have been featured in books and on their covers (see the inside cover of this volume, for example). In 2023, a book dedicated to her art was edited by the eminent curator Necmi Sönmez, whose exhibition *Why Do Poets Draw?* (2022) showcased Sezgener's work alongside seventeen other poets, including Nâzım Hikmet.

ASLI SERİN (Balıkesir, 1977) is a mechanical engineer living in Adana. She has four poetry collections (one cowritten with Birhan Keskin).

ASUMAN SUSAM (İzmir) holds a BA in Turkish language and literature and an MA in film studies. Her poems, surveys, essays, and film criticism appear in numerous journals, edited volumes, and online. She became the first recipient of the Ruhi Su Poetry Award in 2016. English, French, Persian, Hindi, and Spanish translations of her poems have appeared in journals and anthologies. She curated *Oraya Kendimi Koydum* (I Put Myself in Those Shoes, 2023), Turkey's first volume of documentary poetry written by women based on oral histories of women collected by women. She has co-organized symposiums on the influential women poets Didem Madak (1970–2011) and Gülten Akın (1933–2015). Her work on the life and poetry of the latter yielded the edited volume *İncelikler Tarihi: Gülten Akın Şiiri* (History of Subtleties: Gülten Akın's Poetry, coedited with Duygu Kankaytsın, 2022), a biography (2024), and the script for the documentary *Gülten* (2024). She has produced eight poetry collections, three literary surveys, and three edited volumes.

AYLİN ANTMEN (Istanbul, 1981) studies sociology at Istanbul University. Her poems and articles appear in many journals, including *Varlık*, *Cin Ayşe*, *Şiir Ülkesi*, *Damar*, *Özgür Edebiyat*, and *yeni e*. Her first poetry collection was deemed "noteworthy" by the 2008 Yaşar Nabi Nayır Youth Awards. She has published four books of poetry. English translations of her work appear in *Turkish Poetry Today*, Stanford University's journal *Mantis*, and *Circumference Magazine*. She worked as an editor at the publishing house Ve and cofounded Anima Books. Antmen has published many articles at the intersection of psychoanalysis, poetry, and philosophy in *Varlık*.

AYŞEGÜL TÖZEREN (Istanbul) holds an MD from the Faculty of Medicine at Istanbul University. Her criticism appears in many different literary platforms, including *Poetikhars*, *Ücra*, *Dünyanın Öyküsü*, *BirGün Kitap*, and *yeni e*, as well as in the newspaper *Evrensel.* She has served as the deputy editor in chief of *Dünyanın Öyküsü*. Her visual poems were published worldwide in such journals as *Otoliths* and displayed in exhibitions. Her book *Edebiyatta Eleştirinin Özeleştirisi* (Self-Criticism of Literary Criticism) came out in 2018. She collaborates on a health program for Açık Radyo (Open Radio).

BİRHAN KESKİN (Kırklareli, 1963) earned her BA in sociology at Istanbul University. She served as an editor at various literary outlets, including the journal *Göçebe* (1995–98), which she cofounded. Keskin's first poem was published in 1984. Today, she is one of Turkey's most celebrated poets, her books lining the bestseller shelves. Her poems included here were published in her books *Kim Bağışlayacak Beni* (Who Will Forgive Me, 2005), *Ba* (Pa, 2005; winner of the 2006 Altın Portakal [Golden Orange] Poetry Award), and *Soğuk Kazı* (Cold Excavation, 2010; winner of the 2011 Metin Altıok Poetry Prize).

BURAK ACAR (Ankara, 1980) has published poetry in *heves*, *Mahfil*, *Varlık*, *Kitap-lık*, *Japonya*, *Assolist*, *Şerhh*, *Duvar*, *dabaddest*, and elsewhere. His essays and criticism on film appear in *Altyazı*, *Fil'm Hafızası*, and *Sinema Defteri.* He has two poetry collections: *Ateş Akvaryumu* (Fire Aquarium, 2008) and *Tabiat Abi* (Brother Nature, 2018). His book on cinema, *Türk Sinemasında 100 Unutulmaz Karakter* (100 Unforgettable Characters in Turkish Cinema), was published in 2016. He works as a screenwriter and as editor of the prose series Raskol'un Baltası.

BÜLENT KEÇELİ (Konya, 1968–2020) studied chemistry at Selçuk University. He worked as a secondhand bookseller for some time. He cofounded the literary/art journal *Yomsanat* (2001) and, with Murat Üstübal, the poetry journal *Ücra* (2002). He edited for *Ücra* in 2002–5 and 2009–15. Since the late 1990s, his poems and essays have appeared in many journals, including *Kitap-lık*, *heves*, *Kertenkele*, *Kavram Karmaşa*, *Islık*, *Yedi İklim*, and *Karagöz*, and have been anthologized. He coedited a book of interviews with Murat Üstübal in 2019. He published five poetry collections, and his complete poems were published in 2024, four years after his death.

CEM KURTULUŞ (Istanbul, 1985) writes, "I am a filmmaker, community builder, and self-reclaimed *âşık*. I grew up in Istanbul's culturally roaring period of the early 2000s in a disintegrating family of activist dissidents. After losing my mother during high school, I had the privilege to take a detour from performance arts into literary theory and spent a four-year scholarship at Bates College on a double-major BA in English and German. Instead of then following the *script* into academia, I, with the dedication of an avid beginner's mind, established a career in video editing for film and TV while writing/publishing books of poetry, making movies, and building performance stages for the underprivileged in various neighborhoods of New York City. These days I live on the road with my partner, J. F. Vishna, a fellow artist and healer, to simply be here on earth in fulfillment of a vocation, *free as a bird* and in praise of *the refugee*."

CEM UZUNGÜNEŞ (Razgrad, 1962) spent his childhood in a village in Razgrad, Bulgaria, before migrating to Aydın, Turkey, in 1970. He earned his BA in English language and literature at Hacettepe University, Ankara. His poems and essays about poems/poets appear in several journals, and he has four poetry collections. His Turkish translation of Edmund White's book *Rimbaud: The Double Life of a Rebel* (2008) was published in 2017.

CİHAT DUMAN (Elaziz, 1984) grew up in Malatya. After earning his law degree from Istanbul University in 2005, he worked as a lawyer in Istanbul for sixteen years. He immigrated to the United Kingdom in 2023. Between 2010 and 2021, he published two novels and four poetry collections, one of which, *Bir Fil Müddeti* (An Elephant While, 2014), appeared in French translation as *L'espace d'un éléphant* in 2017. He served on the editorial boards of the journals *yeniyazı*, *HurdaSanat*, and *Natama*. He acted in *Wong Kar Wai Üzerine Kısa Bir Film* (A Short Film about Wong Kar Wai, 2014). With Memed Erdener, he co-curated the exhibition *Birbirimizi Hak Edecek Kadar Kötüyüz* (We Are Bad Enough to Deserve Each Other) in 2019. He founded the publishing house Tabiat Kitap in 2022.

DEFNE SANDALCI writes, "I was born, died, and was resurrected (several times) in Istanbul, still lingering in the futurepresentpast, leading a semighosting existence in the city—trying to 'cope' with the late-capitalism catastrophes / horrible gentrification / state terrorism / Turkicization / antisemitism / speciesism / misogyny / ecocide / homo-trans hate / racism / immigrant hate, and and and . . . that fringe groups, communities, individuals, women, men, and animals are subjected to on a daily basis." She has published two books, *Ah!* (2013) and *Aşk İçin İstediğimiz Başka Hayvanlar* (Other Animals We Want for Love, 2020).

DUYGU KANKAYTSIN (İzmir, 1987) holds BA, MA, and PhD degrees in performing arts (dramaturgy) from Dokuz Eylül University. Her doctoral thesis on orientalist tendencies in contemporary Western theater was published as a monograph in 2024. She has published two poetry collections. Her poems have been translated into English, Italian, French, Persian, and Arabic, and she has served as a juror for various poetry prizes. Her essay compilation *Sanatın Gölgedeki Kadınları* (Art's Women in the Shadows, coedited with Özlem Belkıs) was published in 2018. With Asuman Susam, she coedited the volume *İncelikler Tarihi: Gülten Akın Şiiri* (History of Subtleties: Gülten Akın's Poetry, 2022). She co-organized the first Women's Studies Symposium at Dokuz Eylül University in 2016. Kankaytsın's play *Jiyan* ("Life" in Kurdish) received the 2014 Suat Taşer Short Playwriting Award. The radio play *Avludaki Tren* (The Train in the Courtyard), which she adapted from Cemil Kavukçu, was broadcast by TRT Ankara Radio in 2017.

EFE MURAD (Istanbul, 1987) earned his BA in philosophy at Princeton and his PhD in Ottoman history and Islamic philosophy at Harvard, where he's currently a researcher. He has authored six books of poetry and translated ten, including the first complete translation of Ezra Pound's *Cantos* into Turkish, volumes by the American poets Jack Spicer, Tom Clark, Ron Padgett, Susan Howe, and Lyn Hejinian, and a volume by the Austrian author Thomas Bernhard. His bilingual book of poetry, *Breaking of Symmetry/Simetrinin Kırılması* (2022), a collaboration with the quantum physicist Sina Zeytinoğlu and poet-artist Sevinç Çalhanoğlu, was published in a special edition of four hundred, funded by the European Union Grant Scheme for Common Cultural Heritage. One of his recent books, *The Pleasures of*

Empty Lots (2021), is a work of creative nonfiction—a volume of memoristic essays about poetry scenes and flaneurship in Istanbul.

EKİN METİN SOZÜPEK writes, "I see myself as a producer of 'sound' and 'writing.' 'Sound' includes music–dubbing–performance, while 'writing' encompasses literature and the social sciences. During my journey, I received education in theater, film, sociology, economics, public relations, architecture, and meditation. To me, poetry is where an amalgam of all this sprouts. Since I cherish a full-bodied text, I prioritize background sounds and ornaments and generate multilayered weaves by multiplying inner connections. Final word: I was born in Istanbul in 1989."

ELİF SOFYA (Istanbul, 1965) earned a BA in economics and an MBA at Istanbul University as well as an MA in visual arts from Istanbul Technical University. Her artwork has been displayed in various exhibitions, and she has prepared and presented radio programs about art, culture, and politics. She has also edited for television. In 2012, she represented Turkey in the German project "The Poetry of Neighbors—Poets Translated by Poets." She has published four poetry collections, and some of her poems were anthologized in German translation in the collection *In meinem Mund ein Bumerang* (In My Mouth a Boomerang) in 2013.

EMEL İRTEM (Eskişehir, 1969) studied Latin language and literature at Istanbul University and is a retired emergency-room nurse. İrtem's poems, short stories, essays, and interviews appeared in various influential newspapers and literary platforms starting when she was in her early twenties. In 1999, she received the Orhon Murat Arıburnu Award for her poetry collection *Divaneliğe Dönen Pergel* (The Compass Spinning to Insanity), published the same year. She was awarded the Sevda Ergin Award during the 2010 Istanbul International Poetry Festival. She published six more collections of poetry after that. İrtem also has a children's book. Her complete poems were published under the title *Turuncu Travers* (Orange Crosstie) in 2024. Individual poems have been translated into many languages, and a book of selected poetry was published in English translation in 2023.

EMEL KAYA (Nicosia, 1978). Women's nature, as revealed by cultural field research into present-day body politics, lends a powerful undertone to

Kaya's poetry, while women's experience, as it relates to masculine codes and linguistic violence, also manifests itself. Her lyrical-experimental poems, lauded for their originality, exhibit repetitions, ravings, visual effects, spatial fragmentation, mental leaps, and a fairy-tale-like aura. They increasingly contain criticism of the Anthropocene. The three poems featured here by the "sincere and relentlessly self-probing" Kaya, as critics have described her, are steeped in women's imagination and sensitivities, a far cry from the weary words, vehement objections, and rights-seeking images of feminist politics. (emelkaya.com)

EMRAH ALTINOK (Ağrı, 1980) holds a PhD in urban planning from Yıldız Technical University and is currently an assistant professor in the Department of Architecture at Istanbul Bilgi University. In 2003, he received the Rıfat Ilgaz and Melih Cevdet Anday Awards for his first poetry collection. He has two other poetry collections. Under the pseudonym "Franko Buskas," he published the fanzine *gak şiir şeyi*. His rich lexicon draws widely from philosophy, politics, anthropology, sociology, and economics. As Buskas, he has also initiated new collective experiences by creating inscriptions that are part drawing, part handwriting; by audio-recording his poetic ravings; and by installing stencils on walls throughout Istanbul. As an artist, Altınok has exhibited his work in many national and international art venues, including MAXXI (Rome), the Cantieri Culturali Alla Zisa (Palermo), and the Institut français de Turquie. Such outlets as the *Financial Times*, *Die Zeit*, Random House, and Penguin have published his work.

ENİS AKIN (Istanbul, 1964) studied engineering at Istanbul Technical University and in Australia. He published his first poem in 1988. In 1991, he began publishing the fanzine *beyazmanto*, which continues to this day (beyazmanto.com). Since 2013, he's been on the editorial board of the poetry and criticism journal *Natama*. A major figure in the poetry scene in Turkey, Akın has eleven books of poetry, including his collected poems (1988–2019), published in 2023. His prose books include an analysis of Sylvia Plath's poetry, a poetics based on his self-devised concept of "stuttering poetry," and interviews with veteran poets. He has translated the work of the American poets Robert Creeley (2021) and Charles Olson (forthcoming). (enisakin.blogspot.com)

ENİS BATUR (Eskişehir, 1952) is an award-winning writer, translator, and publisher. An eminent intellectual and one of Turkey's most prolific writers, Batur has published numerous books and articles in every genre imaginable (poetry, novel, criticism, essay, diary, travelogue, etc.) since his first book was published in 1973. He's been the editor in chief of Kırmızı Kedi since 2017 and of the poetry journal *Kirpi* since 2020. He was Yapı Kredi Yayınları's editor in chief between 1988 and 2004, during which time it became one of the nation's leading publishing houses. His books have been translated into Dutch, English, French, Italian, Persian, and Spanish. He has won eight awards, including the coveted Cemal Süreya (1993), Altın Portakal (1997), Sibilla Aleramo (1998), and Behçet Necatigil (2008) Awards for his poetry and the Yunus Nadi Award (2018) for his novel *Göl Yazı* (Lake Script, 2017).

ERGUN TAVLAN (Konya, 1959) spent thirty years in Konya and twenty years in New Jersey. He was the coeditor of the e-journal *İmece* between 1998 and 2002. His two books of poetry are *Sesleri Alan:* (Sound Recorded By, 2015) and *Görme Huyu* (Habit of Seeing, 2022). He currently lives in İzmir, where he runs a bookstore.

ERKAN KARAKİRAZ (İzmir, 1974) is a poet, critic, and editor. He has published four poetry collections. He prepares and distributes such fanzines as *Yer Üssü Alfa* and *UBA*. He has worked as editor in chief for a number of print and online literary/cultural journals, including *Kurşun Kalem*, *Caz-Kedisi*, and *Eleştirel Kültür* (ekdergi.com), as well as at the publishing house Pikaresk. He produced, edited, and hosted several episodes of *Turkish Sofa* on Trafika Europe Radio. He cofounded the Açık Şiir (Open Poetry) movement. His interdisciplinary video installations have been featured by the International Istanbul Literature Festival, Exiled Writers Ink, Norwegian PEN, Venice Borders Festival, and İzmir International Literature Festival.

FAHRİ GÜLLÜOĞLU (İzmir, 1975) studied industrial engineering at Dokuz Eylül University. He has been working at Yapı Kredi Yayınları since 2001, where he is primarily responsible for editing Turkish translations of German and English literature. He has published five poetry collections. In 2009, he attended an artist-in-residence program in Vienna thanks to a scholarship from the Austrian Ministry of Culture. In 2016 and 2019, he was invited to stay at the Baltic Centre for Writers and Translators (Visby, Sweden). He does the occasional illustration for book covers. He coscripted the feature-length film *Diyalog* (Dialogue, Ali Tansu Turhan, 2021). He lives in Istanbul.

FATİH KÖK (Keşan, 1985) studied philosophy at Boğaziçi University and Mimar Sinan Fine Arts University. He received the 2017 Arkadaş Z. Özger Award in poetry and the 2018 Fakir Baykurt Short Story Award. His poems, short stories, and essays appear in such journals as *Varlık*, *Yasakmeyve*, *Sözcükler*, *Marşandiz*, and *Bireylikler*. He is a research assistant in the Philosophy Department at Dicle University. His research areas include contemporary ontology, language philosophy, and fiction philosophy. He is also pursuing a PhD in logic at Istanbul University.

FATMA NUR TÜRK (Ankara, 1988) is a poet and translator. She has two poetry collections, *Kargo Kültü* (Cargo Cult, 2016) and *Lady Papa* (2021). She published a Turkish translation of Ted Hughes's poetry collection *Cave Birds* (*Mağara Kuşları*) in 2021. Her translations of Emily Dickinson's poems are slated for publication.

FIRAT DEMİR (Istanbul, 1991) is a Kurdish poet writing primarily in Turkish who has published two poetry collections to much critical acclaim. He edited the Turkish translation of Edmund White's selected stories and of White's biography of Rimbaud, the latter translation undertaken by Cem Uzungüneş (another poet in this anthology). Demir's translation of White's biography of Marcel Proust is the first biography of Proust in Turkish. Demir was commissioned by the Istanbul Biennial to edit an anthology for its thirteenth season in 2013. His poetry and prose have appeared in diverse mediums, such as video art and installation, in collaboration with contemporary artists, and have been exhibited at several biennials and group exhibitions. He has been living in New York since 2014, where he completed his BA in English and comparative literature at Columbia University. He was a recent fellow of the Santa Maddalena Foundation for Writers (Tuscany) and the Residència Literària Finestres (Catalonia).

GONCA ÖZMEN (Burdur, 1982) holds an MA and PhD in English language and literature from Istanbul University. Her honors include the 2003

Berna Moran and 2005 Homeros Criticism Awards. She has published three poetry collections, and translations of her poetry have been published in English (*The Sea Within*, 2011), German, and Macedonian. Individual poems have been translated into nine other languages. She has been invited to international poetry festivals in many countries. She has edited an anthology of contemporary Irish poetry translated into Turkish (2010) and a collection of unpublished poems by İlhan Berk (1918–2008) following the poet's death. Özmen sat on the editorial boards of the journals *Ç.N.*, *Pulbiber*, *Çevrimdışı Istanbul*, and *Turkish Poetry Today* (United Kingdom). She has translated five children's books into Turkish, including one by Sylvia Plath, whose collected poems she is currently translating. She is also busy editing küçük İskender's poetry (see his bio and poems in this anthology).

GÖKÇENUR Ç. (Istanbul, 1971) has seven poetry collections to his name. His honors include the Metin Altıok Poetry Award. Books of his poetry have been published in English, German, Italian, Serbian, Romanian, and Bulgarian. He coedits the Turkish domain of the Poetry International portal and was editor of the literary journal *Çevrimdışı Istanbul.* He's on the editorial board of the Macedonian journal *Blesok*. He has translated poetry from English to Turkish and vice versa and has published books featuring his Turkish translations of works by Wallace Stevens, Paul Auster, Ursula Le Guin, Ocean Vuong, and Anne Carson. He has participated in and organized poetry-translation workshops and festivals in many countries. He's the curator and codirector of Word Express and codirector of the international poetry festivals Offline Istanbul and Poesium Istanbul.

İNANÇ AVADİT (İzmir, 1981) has worked in such disparate areas as tourism, machine operation, field photography, and museum curatorship. His poetry and criticism appear in the journal *Natama* and elsewhere. He has four poetry collections.

KÜÇÜK İSKENDER (1964–2019), literally "Alexander the small," was the pen name used by Derman İskender Över, who studied medicine for five years and sociology for three, completing neither degree. In a heterosexist society, he openly disclosed his homosexuality and his criticism of hypocritical bourgeois moral values, risking humiliation, marginalization, oppression, and violence. His output spanned many genres, including poetry, novel, essay, diary. His poems were anthologized abroad, and he participated in poetry readings, panels, and symposia in Europe and the United States. His books have been published in Kurdish and German translation, and he was the recipient of four awards, including the coveted Melih Cevdet Anday Award (2006) and the Necatigil Award (2017). He often organized poetry gatherings, where he and other poets performed. He also appeared in films, including *Ağır Roman* (Heavy Novel, Mustafa Altıoklar, 1997) and *O Şimdi Asker* (He's a Soldier Now, Mustafa Altıoklar, 2003).

LÂLE MÜLDÜR (Aydın, 1956) studied economics at Manchester University and literary sociology at Essex University. Her poems and writings appear in numerous journals and the newspaper *Radikal.* Some of her poems have been set to music and used in films. She has been published in English (*Water Music*, 1998; *I Too Went to the Hunt of a Deer*, 2008) and French (*Ainsi parle la fille de pluie*, 2002). The recipient of the 2007 Altın Portakal (Golden Orange) Poetry Award, Müldür has on numerous occasions represented Turkey at poetry gatherings abroad. The 13th Istanbul Biennial was named after her book *Anne Ben Barbar Mıyım?* (Mom, Am I a Barbarian?, 1998).

LAURENT MIGNON (Arlon, 1971) is professor of Turkish literature at the University of Oxford and a fellow of St. Antony's College. His research focuses on the minor literatures of Ottoman and republican Turkey, in particular Jewish literatures, as well as on the literary engagement with non-Abrahamic religions, alternative spiritualities, and esotericism in Turkey. He is the author of *Hüzünlü Özgürlük: Yahudi Edebiyatı ve Düşüncesi Üzerine Yazılar* (A Sad State of Freedom: Writings on Jewish Literature and Thought, 2014) and *Uncoupling Language and Religion: An Exploration into the Margins of Turkish Literature* (2021). With Alberto Ambrosio, he coedited the volume *Penser l'islam en Europe: Perspectives du Luxembourg et d'ailleurs* (2021).

LİMAN MEHMETCİHAT (Manisa, 1987) has published poems and writings in many journals, including *heves*, *Ücra*, *Poetikhars*, *Hece*, *Gard*, *Duvar*, *Kargış*, *Başka Dünyalar*, *Kitap-lık*, *Varlık*, and *Pathos.* He cofounded and edited the journals *Sonat*, *Hacı Şair*, *Japonya*, and *Assolist.* In 2019, he founded the online poetry journal *Petroleus.* He has published three poetry collections—interestingly, the third bears an English title, *Killer Instinct of Underdogs* (1987).

MEHMET BUTAKIN (Bingöl, 1979) is a poet, essayist, and critic. He has BA degrees in history and sociology and an MA in international relations. His articles and essays have appeared in newspapers and journals, including *Milliyet Sanat*, *Radikal*, *Varlık*, *Virgül*, *Sanat ve Hayat*, and *Bu Çağ*. In 2001, he received the Yaşar Nabi Nayır Youth Award in poetry as well as the Milliyet Social Sciences Award. He has consulted in the fields of strategic planning and management systems for local governments and has published two poetry collections and a book on political thought.

MEHMET ERTE (İzmir, 1978) is a poet, short-story author, novelist, and editor. He holds a BS in physics. His first poem was published in *Varlık* in 1999. Erte's poems, short stories, essays, and interviews have been published in various literary journals, including *Varlık* and *Kitap-lık*. In 2003, he won the prestigious Yaşar Nabi Nayır Poetry Award for his first poetry collection, published that same year. He has published two additional poetry collections, two short-story collections, and two novels. Erte served as editor in chief of the journal *Yasakmeyve* from 2003 to 2005. He is currently the editor of the publishing house Varlık and of the literary journal *Varlık*, which celebrated its ninetieth anniversary in 2023.

MEHMET CAN İNSPEREST (Ankara, 1991) studied law. He has published poems, prose, and illustrations in various national and international platforms. He coedited the poetry journal *Saydek Şiirsanat*. A collection of his poetry was published in 2016. He currently lives in Ankara.

MEHMET SAİD AYDIN (Diyarbakır, 1983) is originally from Kızıltepe. He lives and works in Istanbul. He studied Turkish language and literature. He has published three poetry collections. The first, *Kusurlu Bahçe* (Flawed Garden, 2011), was awarded the Arkadaş Z. Özger First Book Special Prize and published in French translation as *Le jardin manqué* in 2017. His autobiographical narrative *Dedemin Definesi/Xizîna Bapîrê min/Մեծ Հայրիկիս Գանձը* was published in a trilingual (Turkish, Kurdish, Armenian) edition in 2018. He has also written two pocketbooks on raki gastronomy and translated three books from Turkish to Kurdish as well as various poems from Kurdish to Turkish. He has served as a columnist at *BirGün*, *Evrensel Pazar*, and gazeteduvar.com; prepared programs on the sociology of folk songs on Açık Radyo (Open Radio); and worked as an editor at publishing houses. He is currently working as a scriptwriter.

MERYEM COŞKUNCA (Adana, 1992) studied teaching English as a second language at Bolu Abant İzzet Baysal University. Her first poem was published in the journal *Hayâl.* Later poems appeared in fanzines and the journals *Akatalpa*, *Eliz Edebiyat*, *Gard*, *Lacivert*, and *Varlık.* Coşkunca's first poetry collection won her the Arkadaş Z. Özger Poetry Award in 2016 and was published the same year. Her second poetry collection was published in 2020. Her poems have been translated into English, Persian, Kurdish, and Spanish. She currently lives in Mardin.

METİN KAYGALAK (Bingöl, 1968) studied economics at Uludağ University. His poetry and writings appear in various journals, newspapers, and edited volumes. He was on the editorial board of the literary/art journal *Duvar.* He has published five poetry collections, which were combined into a single volume in 2022. His first poetry collection was published in Kurdish translation in 2005, while individual poems have been translated into English and German as well. Between 2012 and 2013, he presented a cultural program with Pelin Batu on İMC TV, a channel later banned for defending Kurdish rights.

MİRAY ÇAKIROĞLU (İzmir, 1987) has two poetry collections, the first published when she won the Yaşar Nabi Nayır Youth Award in 2014. She collaborated with ten other women poets (including Anita Sezgener, Asuman Susam, and Selcan Peksan, whose poems also appear in this collection) on an edited volume of documentary poetry, *Oraya Kendimi Koydum* (I Put Myself in Those Shoes, 2023). Çakıroğlu translated Philip Larkin's book of poetry *The Whitsun Weddings* (1964) into Turkish in 2021. She researches non-Muslim property in Turkey, focusing on the temporality of the transition from empire to nation-state. She is currently working toward her PhD in anthropology at Stanford University. She holds an MA in Near Eastern studies from New York University. She double majored in English literature and philosophy at Boğazici University.

MURAT ÇELİK (Düzce, 1989) studied Turkish language and literature. He was coeditor of the journals *Habis*, *Sompla Ka*, *Evde Yoktum*, and *Öykülem*. He worked as a copyeditor at the newspaper *Cumhuriyet* and as an editor and publication coordinator at the publishing house Everest. He has four poetry collections (one longlisted for the 2022 Vedat Türkali Award), three short-story collections (one received the 2020 Yunus Nadi Award; another was shortlisted for the 2023 Sait Faik, Haldun Taner, and Türkan Saylan Awards), and a novel. His short story "Fasılasız" was translated into French as "Sans entracte" (Without Intermission) and will be anthologized in 2025. He lives in Istanbul.

MURAT ÜSTÜBAL (Salzgitter, 1968) has an MD from Karadeniz Technical University. His poetry and articles have appeared in journals since 1992. He cofounded the journal *Yomsanat*, coedited the poetry journal *Ücra* with Bülent Keçeli, and served as the theory and criticism editor of the journal *Buzdokuz*. He was the founding editor in chief of the publishing house Heterotopya, which published nineteen poetry books, an essay collection, and a book on contemporary art between 2015 and 2020. Ten poems by five of the poets featured in this volume were drawn from these books. Üstübal has five poetry collections, three essay collections, and a book of interviews, coedited with Bülent Keçeli.

MURATHAN MUNGAN (Istanbul, 1955) spent his childhood and youth in Mardin. He holds an MA in drama (Ankara University) and has worked as a dramaturg. His output spans numerous genres, including poetry, short story, novel, play, screenplay, radio play, essay, survey, and criticism. He has published twenty-two poetry collections, eleven essay collections, fourteen short-story collections, and four novels. Selected works and books have been translated into many languages, including his short-story collection *Cenk Hikâyeleri* (1986), published in English translation as *Valor: Stories* in 2022. His plays and short stories have been staged at such theaters as Schaubühne (Germany), Thessaloniki State Theater (Greece), La Mamma Umbria (Italy), Théâtre des arts de Cergy-Pontoise (France), Bette Nansen Theater (Denmark), and Nottingham Playhouse (United Kingdom). He has participated in numerous readings at home and abroad, and in 2013 he gave the closing speech at the London Book Fair, where Turkey was the theme country. In 2018, he lived in Berlin for a year as a guest of DAAD.

NAZMİ AĞIL (Eskişehir, 1964) earned his BA and PhD degrees in English literature at Boğaziçi University and currently teaches comparative literature at Koç University. The recipient of the 1998 Yunus Nadi Poetry Award, Ağıl has translated into Turkish several canonical works, including *Beowulf*, *Sir Gawain and the Green Knight*, *The Canterbury Tales*, *The Rape of the Lock*, and *The Prelude*. He has nine poetry collections, an academic book titled *Ekfrasis* (Ekphrasis, 2017), and four children's books.

ONUR AKYIL (İzmir, 1980) studied playwriting, dramaturgy, and criticism, earning his BA and MA degrees at Dokuz Eylül University. His first poem was published in 1999. Since then, his poems, essays, and criticism have appeared in various journals and newspapers, including *Birgün* and *Şiirden*. Akyıl has participated in many national and international literature festivals, published twenty books in four genres (poetry, short story, novel, survey), and won five awards, including the 2014 Necati Cumalı Poetry Award. He teaches criticism and drama to various age groups and continues his academic research on anarchism, modernism, antiauthoritarianism, and modern theater.

ÖMER AYGÜN (New York, 1975) is an associate professor of philosophy, teaching at Galatasaray University and specializing in ancient philosophy. He has two books of poetry: *Taş Gün* (Stone Day, 2002) and *Koro* (Chorus, 2010). He has translated works by Sophocles and, with Ari Çokona, Aristotle's *Poetics* (2016). He has also translated French-writing poets, including Rimbaud, Bonnefoy, Michaux, and Ghérasim Luca.

ÖMER ERDEM (Konya, 1967) studied literature at Istanbul University. His first poem was published in the journal *Diriliş*. He cofounded the journal *Kaşgar*. His first book of poetry was published in 1996. He has written numerous reviews and criticism of poetry and poets for the journals *Kitap-lık* and *Varlık*, the newspaper *Karar*, and elsewhere. He has written eleven poetry collections, a book about the life and poetry of Sezai Karakoç, and a collection of essays. Erdem, who has received such honors as the Cahit Zarifoğlu, Fazıl Hüsnü Dağlarca, Attila İlhan, and Oğuz Tansel Poetry Awards, is the father of Nisan and Atlas and lives in Istanbul.

ÖMER ŞİŞMAN (Istanbul, 1980) graduated from the Management and Media Departments at Marmara University. He coedited the poetry journals *Ağır Ol Bay Düzyazı*, *heves*, and *Japonya*. He cofounded and codirected the poetry series Pan-Heves. With Ahmet Güntan, he published the weekly poetry journal *Mahfil*. He has five poetry collections. He manages the publishing house 160. Kilometre, cofounded with Ahmet Güntan and Ali Özgür Özkarcı, which has published more than 150 books of poetry since 2011 (including books by eighteen of the poets featured in this volume).

RIDVAN GECÜ (Istanbul, 1989) earned his BS and MS from Istanbul University and his PhD from Yıldız University, all in metallurgy and materials engineering. He's currently an associate professor at Yıldız University. He has published three poetry collections and a novella.

SELCAN PEKSAN (Sakarya, 1982) is a poet, scholar, and bassist. Of her three poetry collections, one has appeared in English translation: *Slippage* (2022). Also forthcoming is the translation of another poetry collection, *There Is a Cave*. She's a founding editor of the online poetry fanzine *Moero*. An associate professor in the School of Economics at Istanbul University, Peksan also has an academic book to her credit.

SERDAR KOÇAK (b. 1961) writes, "I was born in Eyüpsultan, Istanbul, but grew up in Kalamış. I studied at Maarif Koleji. I've published over forty books in the genres of poetry, narrative, essay, and novel. My first poetry collection *Pervazda* (On the Sill), published in 1991, was also my first book. *Pervazda*, along with *Köhne* (Ramshackle), another of my poetry collections, and my narrative *Ben Napoli Radyosu* (I'm Naples Radio) are among my most beloved works. I'm manic depressive." (Maarif Koleji, or Kadıköy Anadolu Lisesi, as it's currently known, is a well-respected high school, much loved and missed by its many alumni, as evidenced by numerous online posts.)

SERKAN IŞIN (Istanbul, 1976) is among the pioneers of visual and experimental poetry in Turkey. He cofounded the journals *Mizan* and *Buzdokuz*. He also founded the visual poetry journal *Zinhar*, which, after being renamed *Poetikhars* in its online form (poetikhars.com), won the

2009 Türkiye Yazarlar Birliği (Writers Union of Turkey) Digital Publishing Award. His poems, short stories, and articles appear in more than twenty journals, including *Varlık*, *Hece*, *Kitap-lık*, *Yasakmeyve*, *Fayrap*, *Ağır Ol Bay Düzyazı*, *heves*, *Yomsanat*, and *Ücra*. His eight poetry collections were reprinted as a single volume in 2018. His first story, "Ofis" ("Office," 2001), published in *Varlık*, later represented Turkey in an anthology of twentieth-century world fiction published in South Korea in 2002. His visual poems were anthologized in *The Last Vispo Anthology: Visual Poetry 1998–2008* (2012) in the United States and *The New Concrete: Visual Poetry in the 21st Century* (2015) in the United Kingdom. (vedeki.com)

ŞAKİR ÖZÜDOĞRU (Razgrad, 1986) is a contemporary artist and poet. He completed his PhD in communication design and management and his MA in industrial arts at Anadolu University. He has published two poetry collections and various fanzines, e-books, and literary journals. He was the founding editor of the poetry magazine *Gard*, which enjoyed nationwide popularity. He serves on the executive board of the Eskişehir International Poetry Festival. Özüdoğru is a member of the Design and Architecture Faculty at Eskişehir Technical University, and his research interests include contemporary art theory, cultural studies, queer studies, experimental poetry, and postmodern theories.

UTKU ÖZMAKAS (Bergama, 1986) earned his BA, MA, and PhD in philosophy at Hacettepe University. He has translated nearly thirty books into Turkish by such philosophers as Frantz Fanon, Terry Eagleton, Thomas Lemke, Jacques Rancière, Stuart Hall, John Holloway, and Simon Critchley. He is currently working in the Philosophy Department at Düzce University. His books include *Şiirimizde Milenyum Kuşağı* (The Millennium Generation in Our Poetry, 2008), *Şiir İçin Paralaks* (Parallax for Poetry, 2013), *Biyopolitika: İktidar ve Direniş* (Biopolitics: Power and Resistance, 2018), *Prens: Machiavelli'nin Muazzam Muamması* (Prince: Machiavelli's Enormous Enigma, 2019), and *Kartezyen Prens: Descartes ve Siyaset* (Cartesian Prince: Descartes and Politics, 2023).

ÜMİT GÜÇLÜ (Istanbul, 1989) is a poet, critic, editor, and publisher living in Istanbul. He has four poetry collections and a book of poetry criticism. He founded and managed the publishing house Dünyadan Çıkış, which was active from 2017 to 2019. Sometimes he writes slogans on walls with spray paint. He doesn't watch TV. He likes nature, children, basketball, and publishing. He's currently working as an editor at various publishing houses.

YEŞİM ÖZSOY (Istanbul, 1972) is a poet, playwright, director, performer, and producer residing in Istanbul. She has two poetry books. She is the founder and general artistic director of GalataPerform, an Istanbul-based independent theater, focusing on new text, new technologies, and interdisciplinarity. She's also the founder and director of the New Text New Theater project, which has had a leading role in the development of new writing in Turkish theater. With her plays, which have been translated into English and seven other languages, she has attended many festivals nationally and internationally. The play *Yüz Yılın Evi* (House of Hundred), which she cowrote with Ferdi Çetin, was staged at the Edinburgh Festival Fringe in 2019 and selected by *The Guardian* as one of the ten must-sees from among 3,500 candidates. A compilation of her plays was published in 2019.

ZEYNEP KÖYLÜ (Çorum, 1978) has a BA in media and communication from Ankara University and an MA in sociology from Mimar Sinan University. She works as a prompter at the Istanbul Municipality Theater. She was only nineteen when she won the Arkadaş Z. Özger Poetry Award. She was also the recipient of the Orhon Murat Arıburnu Poetry Award in 1999. She has published three poetry collections and participated in numerous literary events and festivals in Turkey and abroad. Her poems have been translated into English, Dutch, Lithuanian, Bulgarian, Italian, and Greek and appeared in various journals and anthologies. She has also coauthored a children's book with Gürçim Yılmaz.

BUĞRA GİRİTLİOĞLU (Istanbul, 1971) founded the queer publishing house obiçim yayınlar in 2021. Through obiçim, he has published thirteen books of poetry and prose by twenty-four authors, including *Bonbon Bönbön*, the Turkish translation of the poetry chapbook *Bun* by Tom Clark and Pulitzer finalist Ron Padgett. In addition to his novel *Çapkın Gezgin'in Ukdeler Kitabı* (Misadventures of a Crush Collector, 2023) and three collections of original poetry (2016, 2019, 2021), his translations appear in *Asymptote*, *Chicago Review*, *Exchanges* (University of Iowa), *Mantis* (Stanford University), *Middle Eastern Literatures*, and *Rusted Radishes* (Beirut). His poems have been translated into various languages. He holds a BS (Cornell) and MS (MIT) in materials science and engineering and an MA in ethnomusicology (Istanbul Technical University). He has taught world music at Boğaziçi University. An avid singer, Giritlioğlu has sung with many choirs in the United States, United Kingdom (BBC Symphony Chorus), Netherlands (Laurenscantorij), and Turkey. He also enjoys playing the piano and oboe. He went vegan in 2012. YouTube: https://bit.ly/2AjfQBL.

DANIEL SCHER (New York, 1967) is a senior editor at McGraw-Hill Education, where he develops interactive technology for K—12 mathematics classrooms. He was the principal investigator of two National Science Foundation grants and is the coauthor of six mathematics texts, including *Explore Mathematics with Origami* (2025). He has taught geometry at New York University and The City College of New York. His website is at sineofthetimes.org.

www.ingramcontent.com/pod-product-compliance
Lightning Source LLC
Chambersburg PA
CBHW030118040325
22763CB00038B/479
* 9 7 8 0 8 1 5 6 3 8 6 2 9 *